MARBLING

For Mum, Dad and Chloe—my biggest and most "marbellous" fans!

This book wouldn't have been possible without the help of some very special people. Thanks to Maureen Duke and Jemma Lewis, my first two masters. To Jo Bryant and Matt Windsor for making sure all my pictures and ramblings have come together in a cohesive fashion. To the talented artists who have allowed me to show off their work. To all those I have pestered to read and review my work. To Tina for encouragement and making me work through lockdown on the lawn. And especially thanks to Alick, who always goes above and beyond, and made this project happen.

Other Schiffer Books on Related Subjects:

20 Projects for Alcohol Inks: A Workbook for Creating Your Best Art, Karen Walker, ISBN 978-0-7643-5646-9

Introduction to Bookbinding & Custom Cases: A Project Approach for Learning Traditional Methods, Tom Hollander & Cindy Hollander, ISBN 978-0-7643-5735-0

Painting with Paper: Paper on the Edge, Yulia Brodskaya, ISBN 978-0-7643-5854-8

Text and photography copyright
© 2020 Freya Scott

Layout and design copyright
© 2020 BlueRed Press Ltd.

Jutta Klee Photography
Pages 6, 11

Emaciated Man on Horse
Rogers Fund, 1944
Page 17

Les Archives Digitales / Alamy Stock Photo
Page 18

Pages 172–174 all images artist's own

All the photography Alick Cotterill

Produced by BlueRed Press Ltd., 2020
Designed by Matt Windsor
Type set in Museo Sans

ISBN: 978-0-7643-6081-7
Printed in Hong Kong

Library of Congress Control Number:
2020941253

Published by Schiffer Publishing, Ltd.
4880 Lower Valley Road
Atglen, PA 19310
Phone: (610) 593-1777; Fax: (610) 593-2002
E-mail: Info@schifferbooks.com
Web: www.schifferbooks.com

For our complete selection of fine books on this and related subjects, please visit our website at www.schifferbooks.com. You may also write for a free catalog.

Schiffer Publishing's titles are available at special discounts for bulk purchases for sales promotions or premiums. Special editions, including personalized covers, corporate imprints, and excerpts, can be created in large quantities for special needs. For more information, contact the publisher.

We are always looking for people to write books on new and related subjects. If you have an idea for a book, please contact us at proposals@schifferbooks.com

MARBLING

Practical Modern Techniques

FREYA SCOTT

SCHIFFER PUBLISHING

4880 Lower Valley Road · Atglen, PA 19310

CONTENTS

To anyone beholding it for the first time it appears extremely simple and easy to perform, yet the difficulties are many and the longer anyone practises it the more he becomes convinced that there is ample room for fresh discoveries and more interesting results than any that have yet been accomplished.

—Charles Woolnough, *The Whole Art of Marbling*, 1853

INTRODUCTION

Marbling is magical—there are no two ways about it. From the mesmerizing flow of the colors on the watery surface, to the apprehensive peeling back of the paper to reveal a pattern, every step of this art has the possibility to be spellbinding. And devastatingly frustrating. Anyone who has ever tried this fascinating process will know the ups and downs, the triumphs and the heartaches, of trying to control myriad elements that *do not* want to be controlled.

Throughout marbling's long history, people have been captivated by both its apparent simplicity and its extraordinary complexity. At heart, marbling is a simple concept—it is the creative act of floating colors on an aqueous surface to manufacture forms and patterns. This is where the simplicity ends, because as I will show throughout this book, there are so many variables in creating marbled art, and as such, it is a unique process to every marbler. No matter how long you have been marbling, there are always new things to learn and obstacles to overcome.

In this book I explain and demonstrate my own way of marbling. This is not necessarily the right way or the best way—but this is what works for me. My hope is that in these pages you will find practical steps and also discover for yourself all its many possibilities. Marbling is both an art and a science—take it as far as you want to go.

MY STORY

There is always a reason people come to art—and no doubt a good reason why you have this book. Although it may seem odd to describe here how and why I first encountered marbling, it is such a part of my drive to continue with the craft (and bookbinding in general) that it would be odder *not* to mention it. Despite my love of books and my bordering-on-the-obsessive fascination with color, I never intended to become a marbler. It was something that happened by accident and then progressed through months and years of focused practice and, frankly, obsession.

My journey into marbling is a peculiar one. I studied art and photography at college and read English literature at university. During my MA year I suddenly became very ill and, instead of improving, kept getting worse. Eventually I was almost housebound. Without a real diagnosis, I was left with no idea of how, or even if, I would ever recover. Aside from extreme fatigue, frustratingly, my cognitive abilities were the most affected. Some days I couldn't even talk properly. I found it difficult to comprehend what people were saying to me—I knew they were speaking English, but beyond that I was in the dark. I lost the ability to concentrate for long periods, and I couldn't read more than a few sentences at once. I'd see the words, but the information never reached home. It was devastating to a student and lover of words and literature.

I was lucky to eventually meet with a health professional who helped me begin to rehabilitate. If I'd known how long

it would take, I might never have started, but I did. Part of my rehabilitation was to find activities and pastimes that would use a different part of my brain from that needed for academia. Within a year or two I had signed up to a couple of arts-based courses in photography and, of all things, bookbinding. I had never heard of bookbinding before, but I loved books, and I had the most impressive array of beautiful notebooks (that I had never written in but was nonetheless entirely in love with), so it seemed a good fit.

That weeklong course set me off on a path I'd never imagined. At the end, I asked the bindery whether I might come in for some work experience. To this day I have no idea why, but they offered me a job instead. I started two days a week,

learning on the job. Since then I have spent nearly a decade working in different binderies and institutions, still learning on the job and recuperating from the illness that threatened to take over my life.

Bookbinding is where I first came across marbled paper. It is such a part of the history of the book that it is impossible not to encounter it. I used it in new bindings; I repaired it in old books; I hunted down replicas for restoration. But for a long time I didn't have any desire to learn how it was done; I was just humbly fascinated by its beauty and by those who had the mysterious skill to produce it. It wasn't until I was working with a charity called Bound by Veterans that I was suddenly called upon to learn it. The charity is a wonderful scheme set up to help veterans learn new skills and rehabilitate, using craft as a form of therapy. I started working with them out of a passion for helping people recover from their illnesses and injuries, and to help them rediscover a part of themselves, just as I had done while learning to bind books. As a part of the course, we arranged for master marbler Jemma Lewis to come in and run a marbling session. It was utterly enthralling. By the end of the day, we each had a stack of beautiful papers that we had made purely from floating paints on thickened water. It seemed somehow ludicrous that these amazing things were possible.

After that first session, I knew our students would want to do more marbling. It would have been lovely to have a master marbler on hand to guide us through the process, but that not being possible, I thought I could be the next best thing. I totally underestimated the level of skill and expertise required! I thought I might pick up enough in a few weeks to be able to run a session, but those weeks turned into months, and the months into years. Those early marbling trials were nothing like that first session. Nothing was behaving the way it was meant to. I couldn't understand it. In some ways it is lucky that I became obsessed with making it work; otherwise I think those first experiments may have killed any desire to keep going.

Marbling is one of the few things that have bewitched me so completely that I have forgotten to eat! I have vivid recollections of standing over my first little tray next to my kitchen sink and poring over it for hours. Family members wandered in and out, making food, getting drinks, passing through: I was oblivious. Before I knew it the day was over, and I'd not touched a morsel. I'd barely started my cup of tea from the morning. Yet, hanging on my little makeshift washing line of string between chairs were a whole array of experiments, mistakes, experiences, all still wet and glistening—some bright and stark, others pale and subtle. It felt like an achievement. It felt like a good day's work.

It still does. I am still captivated by the strange relationship between the intense satisfaction and the extreme frustration that experiments in marbling can produce. Sometimes I do forget lunch. Perhaps I am a glutton for punishment. What I do know is that marbling, and craft in general, is more than just producing something beautiful or functional. It has the ability to reach unseen places. It has the ability to connect people. It has the ability to ground you in a moment. When you begin marbling, that moment can be one of frustration, but perseverance is key; the next moment will be one of elation.

Marbling at its heart is really a form of pattern design, and while there are many things that you can do with marbled paper and fabric, as a bookbinder I love to create books and stationery. There are a few examples on this page showing my use of both materials. I like to turn marbled fabric into book cloth by lining it with Japanese tissue. This ensures the fabric won't stretch and warp when it is applied to the book boards, and that the structure remains strong. Thicker fabrics are ideal for covering files and folders, making them tactile and durable. Any book that has seen better days can be given a new lease on life by being rebound in either paper or fabric, and the beauty of using marbled materials is that everything created will be unique.

Marbling is addictive, and I encourage you to make use of your patterns in whatever way you choose—then go back to the tray, roll up your sleeves, and do it again!

A BRIEF HISTORY OF MARBLING

Marbling has fascinated and intrigued people for centuries, yet even now its origins remain unclear. It appears to have been practiced as early as the twelfth century in Japan, in the form of *suminagashi*, where ink was made to float on water (*sumi* meaning ink and *nagashi* meaning floating). The very earliest examples are seen in the *Sanjurokunin Kashu* ("Anthology of thirty-six eminent poets"), which was presented to the Heian-period emperor Shirakawa in 1113 for his sixtieth birthday. For many hundreds of years this technique remained exclusive to the Japanese imperial household and distinguished nobility. Another form of marbling has its earliest examples originating in late-fifteenth-century Persia and was named *abrī* (from the Persian for clouded paper). This type of marbling used a thickened water substance and heavier pigment paints and is the technique most closely related to the method we use today.

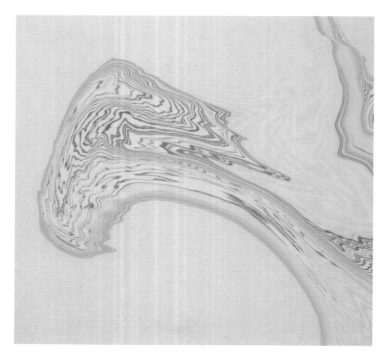

A modern example of *suminagashi* by artist Sarah Amatt.

The thickened water meant that heavier and brighter pigments could be used, and also allowed more control over the paints, which were less apt to wander and eddy than thin inks on water.

It is the general consensus that this form of marbling was developed after the skill of *suminagashi* migrated from East Asia to the Islamic world by way of the trade routes. However, recent research suggests that this method could have been developed in Greater Persia independently of the Japanese technique. Either way, it then grew more prevalent in the region as part of an emerging decorative paper industry centered on Istanbul in the sixteenth century, where the art eventually became known as *ebru* (clouds on water).

These early Turkish marbled papers, although more controlled, were still fairly simple in design, featuring rudimentary spot patterns and wild, swirled designs. European travelers to the region in the late 1500s were excited to discover these colorful decorative papers (which were often termed Turkish papers) and brought them home to be bound into popular *album amicorum* (friendship albums) and other articles. Soon, imported marbled papers began being used across Europe, with examples from the Netherlands seen by the end of the sixteenth century.

The combed, detailed designs that we now associate with traditional marbling seem to first appear at the turn of the seventeenth century. Muhammad Tahir, a Persian artist working in the Deccan region of India, had begun producing highly intricate, combed patterns that eventually won him international acclaim (from *The Art of Abrī: Paper Marbling in the Early Modern Islamic World*, Jake Benson, Leiden University). The use of refined mineral pigments and the advent of patterns such as the chevron are attributed to him, as well as innovative additions to the paints to create special effects

Deccan, mid-17th century. From *Sultans of Deccan India, 1500–1700: Opulence and Fantasy*, by Navina Najat Haidar and Marika Sardar. Published by the Metropolitan Museum of Art, New York, 2015.

Attempts to reconstruct the true history of European marbling are tricky, since very few instructions or accounts about the craft were written down (most marblers worked by passing the skills on from master to apprentice). However, by the middle of the seventeenth century, marbled paper was in common use by English bookbinders, and most papers were imported from France and Germany through the Netherlands. A lot of the patterns dating from this time are even now still referred to as "Dutch."

such as craquelure. His techniques quickly spread from India to Iran and then on to the Ottoman Empire. Soon the repertoire of patterns practiced by abrī artists became seemingly boundless in variety. Samples of these papers—and eventually the techniques to create them—began to travel slowly into Europe.

It is during the seventeenth century that the first English descriptions of marbling occur. In 1628, Francis Bacon described the process in his book *Sylva Sylvarum*, in which he writes that in Turkey "they take divers Oiled Colours, and put them severally [in drops] upon water, and stirre the water lightly; and then wet their Paper (being of some thicknesse) with it; and the paper will be Waved and Veined like Chamolet, or Marble." It is around this time that marbled paper began to be manufactured in western Europe, mainly in France, Germany, and Italy.

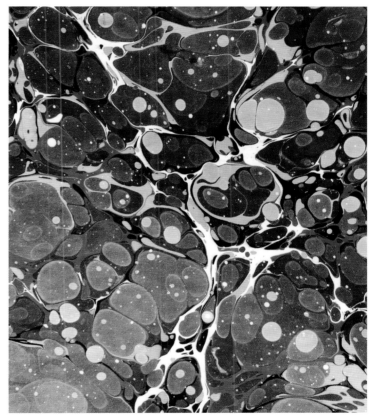

Contemporary reproduction of popular eighteenth-century pattern "Antique Spot" by master marbler Kate Brett of Payhembury Marbled Papers.

Illustration of paper marbling from the *Encyclopédie* by Denis Diderot and Jean le Rond d'Alembert (1771).

It is said that in order to avoid the import tax on these papers, consignments of other articles such as children's toys were wrapped in the paper, which was removed upon arrival in England and sold to bookbinders, who then flattened them for use as endpapers.

Marbling developed slowly in Britain from the latter half of the eighteenth century onward, but practitioners were loath to impart their hard-earned skills to apprentices who may have ended up as competition. There are apocryphal tales of marbling houses partitioning their workshops with wooden screens, and teaching their apprentices only one aspect of the craft each: how to grind colors or how to make a specific pattern, or how to prepare the *size*. In fact there are tales of

marbling houses with blacked-out windows, and any hole or crevice stuffed up so no one might peer in and purposely (or inadvertently) learn the mystery of marbling.

This veil of secrecy was finally lifted in 1853, when an Englishman named Charles Woolnough described the entire process in his book *The Whole Art of Marbling*. Many marblers were outraged that their centuries-old professional secrets were finally open to the world, but it led to an increased interest in the craft, and more practitioners across Europe and the United States. Eventually other handbooks on the subject were published, one of the most famous being Josef Halfer's *The Progress of the Marbling Art* in 1885. Sadly, by the time bookbinders had their hands on these coveted

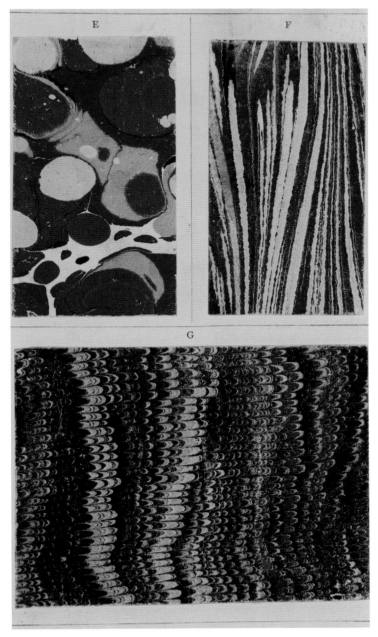

Renowned bookbinding firm Zaehnsdorf included a chapter on marbling in their book *The Art of Bookbinding*, published in 1890.

The Whole Art of Marbling by Charles Woolnough not only included information on tools and materials but also contained step-by-step guides to making patterns.

recipes, the world of book production was rapidly changing. Fine craftsmanship was being replaced by the high-volume print run, and printing methods meant that other forms of decorative paper were on the rise. Cheaper, mass-produced cloth-bound books meant that the comparatively expensive hand marblers found themselves with little employment, and most businesses eventually disappeared.

There were pockets of revival throughout the twentieth century, yet even now at the time of writing, marbling in Britain still remains on the Heritage Craft Association's "Red List of Endangered Crafts." However, with increased ability to share work and information via modern technology, and the renewed interest in arts and crafts for recreation, increasing numbers of people are taking up this centuries-old art form. Although the materials may have changed, modern marbling still employs many of the skills learned and performed by the very earliest practitioners.

TOOLS AND MATERIALS

Before you begin marbling, you'll need to collect together some tools and materials as listed below. To begin, you don't have to have any specialist kit at all, but as you progress you may want to add some of the optional patternmaking tools. Everything listed here—aside from blender, gloves, drying rack, and wooden boards—is explained in greater detail in this chapter.

TOOLS/EQUIPMENT

Blender or mixer for making *size*
Drying rack
Latex or rubber gloves
Paint applicators: whisks, brushes, pipettes, eye droppers
Pots or jars for mixing paint
Rakes and combs—optional
Styluses
Tray(s)
Wooden boards larger than paper size

MATERIALS

Alum
Paint
Paper
Size (the aqueous substance in the tray to marble on)—carrageenan or methocel

TOOLS

Most of the tools needed for marbling are fairly simple and easy to get hold of. I have given examples of substitutes you can make and where you can make things yourself. Bear in mind that you should particularly avoid detergents when washing tools and equipment, since these can have a negative effect on how your paints work.

TRAY

Most marblers will use either a specially built marbling tray with a reservoir and drying board, or an aluminum or stainless-steel tray, which are usually custom-made. The tray you choose to begin with can be anything that will hold liquid—you can use a baking tray, a plastic document tray, or even a gardening tray. A shallow tray about an inch deep will be easiest to use for your marbling bath. Choose one with square rather than rounded corners (although this is not strictly necessary). It is also worthwhile getting a smaller tray for testing the colors before you begin, so you don't contaminate your main tray. This tray should ideally be about 12 x 10 in., since this will best mimic the surface tension of your main tray. It should contain the same *size* as used in your main tray.

PAINT APPLICATORS

There are many ways of applying paint to your *size*, and each one will give you a different effect and release differing amounts of paint. Again, this is a great chance to experiment!

Whisk is the name given to a rudimentary marbling brush that is often made from natural broom straw. They are great at delivering an even layer of paint quickly over the *size*. Whisks may be purchased from marbling supply companies or made from scratch—simply gather a bunch of broom straw and secure one end with a rubber band. Cut the ends flush and there you have it, a whisk! These are especially good for use in watercolor marbling, though there is no reason why they can't be used for acrylics or oils too. For my acrylic paint work, I've made a selection of whisks from plastic broom bristles instead, since they are longer lasting and easier to clean.

Brushes: When it comes to these, there is a seemingly endless choice. Traditional Turkish marblers use brushes made from horsehair that is then bundled around one end of a stick

of rosewood. These can be bought online from specialist marbling-supply companies and are often imported from abroad. By far and away the easiest option is to buy cheap, stiff-bristled paintbrushes in an array of sizes and experiment with them. Try anything, from artists' brushes to house paintbrushes to even makeup brushes!

Eyedroppers and **pipettes** come in all shapes, sizes, and materials and are great for controlling exactly where you want a drop of paint to fall. Thanks to this particular quality, they are used mostly for regular, regimented patterns. However, there's no reason why you can't use a dropper for irregular patterns too—in fact, some marblers take things a step further and put their paint in dropper bottles. These can be shaken at random over the *size* to give large-scale coverage quickly.

STYLUSES
Almost anything will make a good stylus. I've used bamboo sticks, needles, chopsticks, awls, the wrong end of a paintbrush—all these things create different effects in the marbled patterns, so I encourage you to have a go and see what works for you!

CONTAINERS
You will need an array of paint pots or jars for mixing colors. Depending on the type of paint and the amount you are mixing up, these can range between anything from plastic shot glasses to large glass jars. You can even go for an ice cube tray, or a muffin pan.

RAKES AND COMBS

Pictured here are an array of marbling tools called rakes and combs. You'd be forgiven for thinking that this was the start of a peculiarly medieval arsenal, but these are the everyday bits of equipment used for making some of the most beautiful and delicate marbled patterns imaginable. You'll see different sizes and how they can be used in the "Patternmaking" section.

Most marblers make their own tools, since they have to fit the size of their tray exactly. There are many ways of creating your own marbling tools. The tools featured here are treated wood with stainless-steel pins sunk into them.

HOW TO MAKE A RAKE OR COMB

It is worth making your own tools so that they exactly fit the size of your tray. There are many ways to make a rake (or comb), depending on your level of skill. For a beginner's tool, try a strip of heavyweight cardboard with dress pins stuck through, or try taping cocktail sticks to a bit of board. You can even hammer tacks into a piece of wood for a rudimentary rake. For something with a little more longevity, you'll want to use wood and some steel pins or tacks. I make all my rakes and combs with stainless-steel pins so they won't rust, and they all look a little different! However, here are some basic instructions on making a simple but strong comb from wood and pins.

1. Cut two pieces of thin wood the width or length of your tray.

2. Mark on one piece the intervals at which you want your pins to be set, perhaps every 0.25 in.

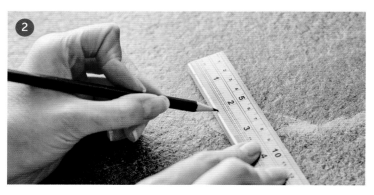

3. Using a glue gun or other waterproof adhesive, stick T pins where you've marked the wood, and let it dry.

4. Apply a second layer of glue and attach the second piece of wood over the T pins.

5. The finished comb. Once dry, you can paint the whole thing with a waterproof coating.

6. Alternatively you can cut a single piece of wood, mark it up, and drill holes the diameter of your pins. Insert the pins, using a bit of glue to hold them in place, and coat with a waterproof covering. This is especially useful for making a bouquet comb as used on page 88. A bouquet comb is made up of two staggered rows of pins in a triangular pattern. The image above shows a 1-inch bouquet comb.

As you become more proficient in marbling, you will get to learn what you need from your rakes and combs. Some can be made that will fit both sides of the tray: by length it fits the long side, and then on the short side the pins overhang the edge of the tray. You can also make rakes and combs that have shoulders that sit on the edge of your tray as you use them. But if you are going to do this, make sure that your pins are not going to touch the bottom of your tray as you use the comb!

MATERIALS

The following pages will take you through the details of all the materials you'll need when you start marbling. It is worth mentioning here, however, that all materials are affected in some way by the environment you choose to marble in. People have actually done research into the ideal environment in which to marble, but unless you are lucky enough to have a vacuum-sealed, spotless, climate-controlled laboratory to marble in, chances are you will have to make do with whatever space you have and whatever climate fate provides.

I have read in various places that the optimum temperature for marbling is anywhere between 64°F and 72°F. While I can attest to the truth of this, I should also point out that at no point in my marbling career have I been able to dictate the temperature in any of my classrooms or studios except for cranking up the radiator in winter and opening the windows in summer. It has been anywhere from 50°F to 95°F in the spaces I've worked in, and believe me, both ends of the temperature spectrum cause their own very special marbling issues. For experiments, changes in temperature can yield some really interesting results, but if you are looking for consistency,

you are best off trying to hover around those optimum temperatures, and making sure that your materials (paints and *size*) are also at the same temperature.

Humidity can also be an issue. If your environment is too dry, paints can have trouble spreading, and both the surface of the bath and the paints can dry very quickly. If you think humidity might be the cause of a problem and you intend to marble regularly, it may be worth investing in a humidifier. Alternatively, misting the air with water from a spray bottle can help.

You will find that a lot of the recipes in this section call for distilled or softened water. This is because the minerals and pH of tap or hard water can have a negative effect on your marbling materials. And you should use the same water for mixing all your materials. This doesn't mean that hard water won't work at all, but it could play a part in causing marbling problems. By using distilled or softened water, you will at least have eliminated one source of potential problems.

It is also a good idea to keep your marbling environment as free from dust as possible, especially when marbling with watercolors and gouache. Dust particles, even fibers from clothes, can fall onto a pattern and cause small holes and irregularities. Of course, it is impossible to remove all sources of dust, and occasional imperfections must be expected, and in some ways these even add to marbling's handmade charm.

The age of your marbling bath will also have an influence on how your paints behave. You can use these effects to your advantage as you learn about what your *size* does throughout its lifespan. For example, some marblers prefer to make certain patterns when the *size* is fresh, since the paints behave in a way that best fits how that pattern is made. Another marbler might like to make that same pattern on an old bath because

that best fits their style. A lot of marbling is unique to the individual and their own methods and practices.

Finally, please don't let this introduction put you off. Marbling is a balancing act, and chances are you may encounter only one or even none of the problems listed here. If you don't intend to marble regularly or you aren't that worried about producing the perfect print, very little of this will apply to you, but the information is here should you ever need it! There are more troubleshooting tips throughout this section, and in the troubleshooting sections on pages 35, 49, 56, and 166–171.

MAKING *SIZE*

The word "size" refers to the thickened water that the paints are applied to and float on for marbling. Most *sizes* throughout the centuries have been sourced from various types of plant matter either dissolved or boiled in water to release its mucilage (a gelatinous polysaccharide substance). Popular bases for marbling have included *sizes* made from tragacanth, fenugreek seeds, and linseed. However, since Josef Halfer's 1885 book, the most popular choice has been (and, for a lot of marblers, still is) carragheen, a seaweed also known as Irish moss. Once you would have had to boil down quantities of the dried moss and then strain it several times through colanders and muslin in order to obtain a thick liquid for marbling. Now, thankfully, you can obtain an extract of the moss called carrageenan, which comes in powdered form and only needs blending with water to create a decent *size*. It is important to note that not all forms of carrageenan will work. It is used in the food industry as a thickener in anything and everything from ice cream to toothpaste, and there are several grades of carrageenan, but only one will work for marbling. It is called lambda carrageenan and is sold mostly by marblers and specialist art stores. You can sometimes find carrageenan in health food stores, but often these are of the types kappa or iota. Neither will work for marbling, since they eventually thicken to form jellies and won't allow your paints to spread well.

The excellent thing about a carrageenan *size* is that you can use any type of paint on it. Originally it would have been used with water-based paints similar to watercolors, but now it is used with gouache, acrylics, oils, and even some dyes and inks. It is ideal for the creation of fine, combed patterns.

The downside is that carrageenan is expensive and does not last that long. It is spoiled easily by some paint types (notably acrylics) and has a tendency to break down over time, changing its consistency and (unfortunately) its smell, both of which are accelerated by warm temperatures. Having once left a tray in my studio for a week during a warm summer spell, I can attest to the fact that old carrageenan *size* smells worse than a seaweed-covered beach at low tide in the midday sun!

Another option is a methocel *size*, a mixture of water and methylcellulose—a wood pulp extract. This is most suitable for acrylic marbling and has the advantage of lasting a lot longer and being less likely to spoil. It is especially good for fabric marbling. Again, there are several different types and grades; the commonest for marbling is known as CMC. It is always best to buy marbling methocel that comes with its own instructions, but the recipe here has worked for me with the several types I have used.

CARRAGEENAN *SIZE*

When in powder form, carrageenan should be kept in an airtight container and away from extremes of temperature. In this state it can last for years. Once mixed, the *size* will last between two and three days, but it can also be refrigerated for about a fortnight to extend its lifespan. It can even be frozen. When you want to use it, leave it to defrost until it reaches room temperature before marbling.

The *size* is very important—if it isn't right, none of the rest of your marbling session will go smoothly. Whenever I am having a marbling issue, the first thing I question is my *size*, and often it is the culprit. The best way to avoid issues is to make sure you start with either distilled or softened water. Believe me—the effort is worth it!

There are many different recipes for the ratio of carrageenan to water. Here are some basic instructions and a rough recipe for making carrageenan *size*. The only reason it is a "rough" recipe is that, being a natural product, every batch of carrageenan is different. I have sometimes had two different bags on the go and, using the same recipe, have had completely different consistencies. This is a base on which you can build. As an organic product, once you've finished with it, the carrageenan can be disposed of down the drain, swooshed away with lots of water.

What you will need to mix carrageenan *size*:

• Lambda carrageenan powder
• Old blender or an electric hand mixer / whisk
• Tablespoon measure
• Tray
• Water (ideally distilled or softened).

Recipe:
1 tablespoon carrageenan powder to 2 pints of water

1. Using an old blender or food processor, add 1 tablespoon of powdered moss to roughly 2 pints of very hot water—use the hottest water your blender can handle. Mix at a very high speed for 30 seconds to a minute, or longer if it's not mixing. Sometimes it helps to start the blender first and add the powder through the top. If you are using a hand mixer, you will need to mix vigorously until there are no lumps remaining. This is very important since you want to end up with a really smooth *size*, free of any clumps. If you are in any way unsure about whether you have a smooth consistency, you can always strain it through a fine sieve or cloth.

2. Pour the *size* into your tray and continue until you have the desired amount and depth.

3. Ideally, leave the *size* lightly covered overnight to cool and for the bubbles to dissipate.

4. On the day of marbling, thin the *size* with lukewarm water to the consistency of thin olive oil—slightly thicker than milk but not as gloopy as oil. Leave to come to room temperature before beginning.

5. These are the basic instructions for mixing carrageenan *size*. The *size* will thicken as it cools. However, if when mixing it the liquid seems extremely watery, reduce the amount of hot water for the remaining powder. When cooled, if the consistency seems too thick, add more water to the tray and reduce the ratio of powder to water when you next marble.

METHOCEL *SIZE*

Usually a cheaper alternative to carrageenan, methocel works brilliantly for acrylics. You will also find that it does not need to be refrigerated and will last a lot longer before spoiling. Once again, it's best to use distilled or softened water and to follow any instructions that come with the powder. In the absence of any directions, the following recipe works for me and can be thinned down if made too thick. Once finished with, the *size* can be disposed of down the drain with lots of water.

What you will need to mix methocel *size*:

- Methocel powder
- Mixing bowl or other container
- Tablespoon measure
- Tray
- Water (ideally distilled or softened)

Recipe:

Roughly a US tablespoon to a US pint (1.5 Imp. tbsp./litre) of water. Half the volume hot, half cold.

1. Work out how many pints you will need for your tray, then add the required amount of methocel powder to your mixing bowl or container.

2. Mix the powder with the half of hot water. Stir until the powder has been well dispersed.

3. Add the remaining half of cold water. Stir gently until thoroughly well mixed.

4. You do not need to wait long to use a methocel *size*—let it stand until it becomes clear and smooth and has reached room temperature (often less than an hour, but it won't hurt to be left longer).

5. Add more water if the *size* needs to be thinned. It should be roughly the consistency of olive oil—slightly thicker than milk, but different paint types and brands will require different consistencies, and this is a matter of trial and error.

Some instructions for methocel call for only hot water, or only cold. Some require ammonia and vinegar to be added—the former helps the methocel dissolve by turning the water alkaline, and the vinegar brings it back to a neutral pH. I have never found the need for this, but it is worth considering if you find your methocel will not dissolve. If this is the case, add 2.5 US tablespoons of ammonia to every 8.5 US pints (2 Imp. tbsp. / 4 litres) of water. Once your methocel has dissolved, add 2.5 US teaspoons (2 Imp. tsp.) of white vinegar to bring it back to neutral.

SKIMMING—CLEANING THE *SIZE*

Before testing your paints or beginning to marble, it is extremely important to skim the surface of your *size*. Not only does this remove any air bubbles or detritus that has fallen onto the bath, but it also has the effect of improving the surface tension by removing the thin film that is caused by the imperceptible drying of the *size*.

Using strips of newsprint (or newspaper) the width of your tray, lay the strip mostly flat on the surface while holding a little of the strip clear of the *size*. Drag it across the surface from one end to the other, being careful to pull the strip up the side of the tray and out. Don't press down on the strip as you pull it— you don't want to accidentally push anything under the surface of the *size* that might lead to contamination later.

You may need to do this a few times to clear the surface to begin with. You will also need to skim after every pattern to remove any excess paint, as well as dirt and air bubbles, before you start the next pattern. Your best results will come when you throw paint for the next pattern immediately—literally seconds—after the last skim.

TIP: Keep notes in a journal about the type, make, and amount of size powder you use each time—and the outcome. This will be very useful for future projects. In fact, keep notes about everything you use and do!

Troubleshooting—Making *Size*

My size *has lumps in it:* If you used a blender for carrageenan *size*, you may not have blended it for long enough or used hot-enough water. If making methocel, refer back to the instructions and make sure you have used either hot or cold water as directed, and make sure you stir until the powder has fully dispersed and dissolved. You can also strain your *size* by using a fine sieve or cloth.

My size *is too thick:* Thin your *size* down, using lukewarm water until it has reached the desired consistency. Leave it to come to room temperature before using. Next time, adjust your water-to-*size* ratio to make it less thick. Keep doing this and make frequent notes until you find the best ratio for your particular brand or batch of *size* powder.

Size is too thin—I've accidentally *thinned it too much by adding water:* You can't add more powder into *size* that has already been made. If it's too thin from the recipe you have used, you will need to make more *size* and adjust the ratio of powder to water to make it thicker. Be sure to keep notes on what you do, and be aware this may change again if you move onto another brand or another batch. If you have overly thinned your *size* with water, there's not much you can do to thicken it up again except make more. Sometimes it is a good idea to hold back a bit of thicker *size* when first making up your tray, just in case you accidentally thin it down too much. You can then add the thicker *size* into your tray to bring it to the correct consistency.

I don't know if I have the correct consistency: This is a tough one when you first begin to marble. There are no hard-and-fast rules, and it is something you will have to learn through experience. As a rule of thumb, the consistency of olive oil—slightly thicker than milk—is a good place to aim for. The way your paints behave will also help you learn. Just be sure that whatever changes you make, make a note of it for next time, so you can replicate it or avoid it!

Sometimes paint will slip beneath the surface of your *size* and either sit on the bottom of the tray or make it appear muddy and dirty. This is to be expected, especially after a long marbling session. Try to skim only in one direction and keep only one end of the tray as the "dirty" end. Sometimes paint will sit on the very bottom of the tray. Ideally paint shouldn't do this, but don't be worried if it happens at times (you can find tips on how best to avoid this in the "Mixing Gouache and Watercolor Paint for Marbling" section, starting on page 45). As long as your newsprint strips are coming off the surface clean, the *size* is good to marble on. The paint on the bottom will eventually add to the spoiling of the bath, but as long as there isn't too much, it should last a good long time!

At some point your *size* will reach the end of its lifespan. You will know this either by smell (in the case of carrageenan), consistency, or the fact that the paints just won't work in the same way anymore. At this point there is nothing to do but throw the *size* away and start again.

PAPER

CHOOSING PAPER

Lots of different types of paper will marble. Your choice will often depend on your budget and the final use of the paper. Here are a few things to consider:

• **Quality**—Ideally you want a strong, good-quality paper that has a good wet strength. This means it will withstand rinsing and can hold its own weight when hung up to dry. Cheap paper is likely to be thin and poorly made. Printer paper, for example, disintegrates easily when wet.

• **Weight**—There really is no hard-and-fast rule for the best weight of paper to marble on, especially since two separate paper types of the same weight can sometimes look and feel very different indeed. The key here again is strength. Some very

thin handmade papers will marble very well because of the way the long fibers are randomly interwoven. Very thick or heavy papers tend to be harder to lay on the surface of the marbling bath and are more prone to catching air bubbles. In general, papers between 80 and 160 gsm are the easiest to marble with.

• **Finish**—Uncoated papers work best for marbling. Watch out for any paper that is coated or has a sizing, since you will probably find the paint will not adhere well. It is possible to marble onto textured paper, but be aware of internal sizing in some papers, since this will also prevent the paints from sticking properly.

• **Intended use**—This can often dictate what type of paper you choose. For example, as a bookbinder and bookbinding supplier, I find that a lot of my papers are of a weight and finish that will allow them to be easily used for endpapers and coverings. A few brands worth trying are Fabriano, Canson, and Daler Rowney, all of which are available in sheets and pads from good art stores. It is worth going to a good art or paper store so you can see and feel different papers. Or find an online supplier that will send you small samples of paper to test and play with. There are a few suppliers listed in the back of this book that I recommend, but at the same time I also encourage you to just play with whatever you like and can get hold of. Try textured paper or even colored paper. Some papers will work, some won't, but as you will no doubt find out, a lot of marbling is trial and error, and discovering your favorite paper to marble on is all part of the fun!

PREPARING PAPER FOR MARBLING

The marbling techniques used in this book require you to prepare your paper with a mordant before use. A mordant is a substance that helps fix a dye or pigment to a surface. In the case of paper and fabric marbling, the mordant forms a bond both with the paint and the fibers of either the paper or the fabric, allowing the marble pattern to stick while the material is rinsed. If you don't do this step, you'll find that you create some very beautiful patterns that look stunning for a second— before all the paint starts to slide off.

The substance I use to prepare my materials is called aluminum potassium sulphate, or alum for short. It is easily found online or in good art stores and is relatively inexpensive. It comes in the form of a powder, small crystals, or large, rocklike pieces. All forms work, but I prefer the small crystals. They dissolve easily in water and seem less apt to re-form once in solution. I make up a fresh batch for every marbling session. When preparing and using alum, it is important to wear gloves, because it can dry and irritate the skin.

What you will need to make alum:

- Aluminum potassium sulphate powder or crystals
- Bowl or open container
- Hot water
- Jug
- Weighing scales

Recipe:

1 oz. of alum to 38.5 fl. oz. of water (30 g / 0.5 Imp. pint). These amounts can safely be halved or doubled.

1. Measure 1 oz. (30 g) aluminum potassium sulphate and put it into a bowl or other open container.

2. Add 38.5 fl. oz. (0.5 Imp. pint) of freshly boiled water.

3. Stir gently until all the alum has dissolved.

4. Leave to one side to cool to room temperature before using.

COATING PAPER FOR MARBLING

All marblers will coat their papers slightly differently and use them at a different stage of dryness. It is possible to coat a lot of papers in advance and keep them for a future session. Some marblers keep theirs for years in a sealed bag or folder, and they come out as fresh as the day they were coated. I always like to make mine up fresh an hour or so before I want to use them, when they are just dried and flat.

What you will need to coat paper:

• Alum solution
• Newsprint or blotting paper—optional
• Paper
• Sponge or large soft paintbrush
• Wooden boards larger than the paper being used

1. Mark the back of your paper with a penciled *X* or initials if marbling a number of papers—once dried, it is difficult to tell which side has been coated with alum. One of the worst feelings is putting your paper wrong-side down onto your freshly made pattern and then having to watch the paint slide off!

2. Lay the paper front-side up on a table in front of you. Using a sponge (a soft, round baby sponge is ideal for this) or a large, soft paintbrush, apply a thin layer of alum as evenly as possible across the whole paper. The aim is not to soak the paper all the way through, but equally, enough should be applied to cover the paper without leaving dry areas.

3. Put the sheet to one side. Repeat step 2 with another sheet. Once coated, you can lay the second sheet on top of the first, alum side up.

4. Keep going until you have coated all the papers you need.

5. I like to leave the papers to air-dry until they are just slightly damp, or still cold and pliable. Then they are stacked, ten sheets at a time, between wooden boards, where they finish drying while being kept fully flat. You can flatten more at a time, but the more sheets, the slower the drying time.

6. You may find that the type of paper you are using needs some extra help to dry. You can sandwich each of your coated papers between pieces of newsprint or blotting paper before stacking them under boards. This extra newsprint or blotting paper will help absorb any excess moisture quickly. If you want to really speed up the process, you can stack your sandwiched papers singly between separate boards.

7. Before using your paper, check it all over for damp spots. Wet alum will not allow paint to adhere. Check it also for smoothness—a sandy feeling is a telltale sign that too much alum was used, and it has begun to re-form into crystals on the surface of the paper. These crystals can transfer to your marbling tray when the paper is laid down, and will eventually contaminate it.

PAINT

One of your most important choices will be the type of paints you use. In theory, you should be able to use any kind of paint or ink to marble with, as long as you can make it float and spread. For example, you can use oil paints, fabric paints, and inks, as well as acrylics and watercolors. This book deals specifically with the last two, since they give the marbler the most control over their paints and allow for the most delicate and detailed patterns.

It is important to remember that not all paints are created equal! Some paints work better than others, and all of them have their own unique behavioral properties. Even within a particular paint type or brand, there's no one rule to paint mixing. This, believe me, is one of the joys (and the frustrations!) of marbling. The trick is to balance the colors —and your *size*—so that both work together in complete and lovely harmony.

It is worth noting here that whatever tools and trays you choose to use for marbling, you will need to keep each type of paint and tools separate from each other. Residue from acrylic paints in your tray or on your tools may contaminate the *size* and have a negative effect on your results if you use them when marbling with gouache or watercolor. Some amazing experimentation can be done when mixing paint types, but be prepared for some serious cleaning effort afterward if you want to be able to use the tray or tools again!

If you do choose to dabble with oil-based paints, it is best done in completely separate trays, using separate tools and brushes/whisks. There are some great books and tutorials on oil marbling out there. Oil marbling can be done on plain water as well as on a thickened *size*, but either way there is generally less control over the paints. They also need to be thinned with turpentine, and all tools and trays need to be thoroughly cleaned afterward with rubbing alcohol.

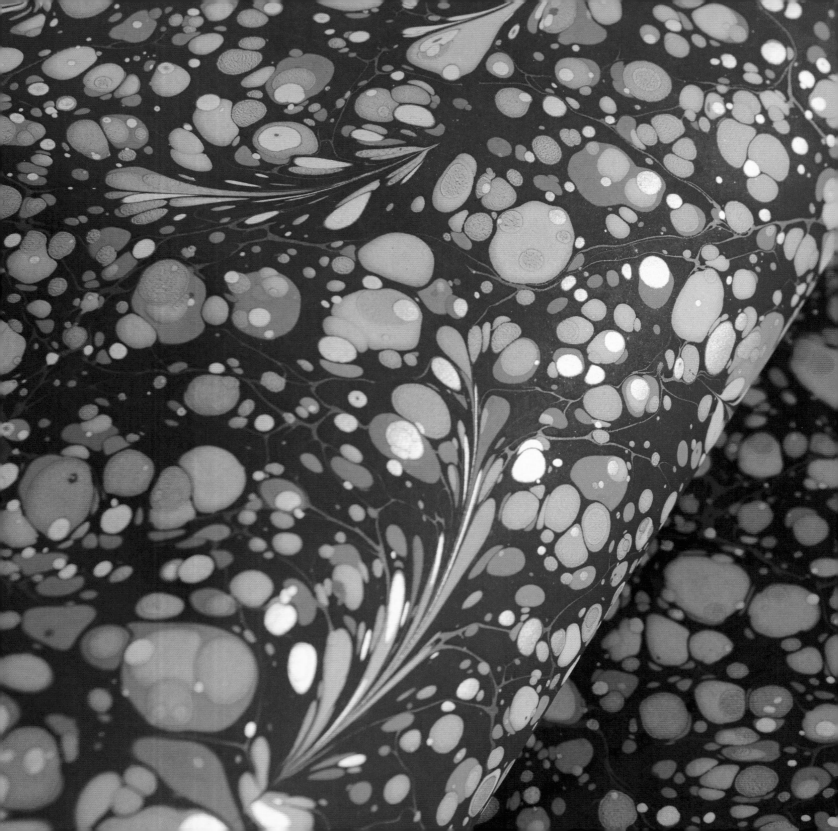

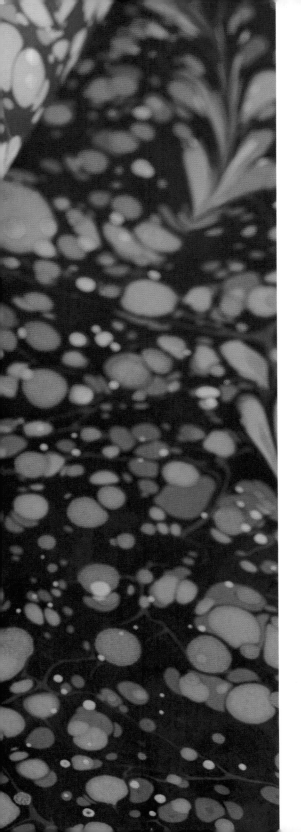

GOUACHE AND WATERCOLOR MARBLING

Watercolor marbling is often described as the hardest and most temperamental form of the art. It is well known among seasoned marblers that delicately balancing the relationship between the materials and the environment is the key to the success of marbling with this medium. It seems that everything from the humidity and temperature of the space to the temperature and pH of your materials can play a part in deciding whether the process is straightforward or troublesome. At times you will question whether your water is really all that soft. You'll start wondering if the cold weather isn't the thing responsible for those weirdly shaped blobs of paint. You may find yourself at times toying with the idea of leaving an offering in your tray for the marbling gods. Yet, despite some of the inevitable (and truly annoying) difficulties, watercolor and gouache marbling can allow the artist scope to produce some of the finest, crispest, and most intricate of marbled patterns.

When working with watercolors, you'll want to use the kind that are found in tubes and not the kind that come in pans. As with all other paints, those with a high pigment content will give you the best results and the brightest colors. Look for professional ranges rather than student paints. I have had success with Winsor & Newton, Daler Rowney, and Sennelier.

Gouache is a fantastic medium—in essence, it is an opaque watercolor. In fact the word "gouache" is a French word that is derived from the Italian word *guazzo*, which means watercolor. The main difference between the two is that gouache has a higher pigment-to-binder ratio (which allows solid, vivid colors even when thin and watered down), and it has an added white pigment (most often chalk) to make it opaque. It also has the added bonus of being very easy to clean up after you've spattered your walls/table/hands/arms with it, since it washes off with water.

It is best to choose a good-quality gouache to marble with. Aim for something with a high pigment-to-binder ratio. Often this will mean looking toward the more expensive brands. However, you will end up using less paint and will get better, brighter results than settling for a cheaper alternative, thus making the outlay worthwhile. Again, search out the professional or designer ranges for the best results. These ranges usually have a selection of exciting metallics too.

You need to buy only a few paints to start with, since you can easily mix them. However, I always advise new marblers to use the colors straight from the tube to begin with, until you get a feel for how they behave. All colors have their own behaviors due to their unique binders and pigments. Mixing them without knowing their qualities means you can end up with some very confusing results, and you won't know which paint is the culprit!

When marbling with watercolor and gouache, you will need to use a carrageenan *size*, since these paints will not work well on methocel.

MIXING GOUACHE AND WATERCOLOR PAINT FOR MARBLING

What you will need:

- Brush
- Dispersant—ox gall or dilute detergent
- Paint
- Pipette(s)
- Pot or container
- *Size*—carrageenan
- Water—soft or distilled

Unless you are using ready-mixed marbling watercolors, any paint straight from the tube will need thinning with water. Once thinned, most will also need help to spread on the surface of the marbling bath. To do this, use a dispersant. Traditionally, the additive used is ox gall, which is exactly what it sounds like—bile from the gall bladder of a cow. It acts to help the paint break the surface tension of the *size*, and also to stop colors running into each other.

These days it's possible to acquire ox gall online or from specialist stores. You can use the ox gall that is meant for use in watercolor painting, but often this is too weak for marbling purposes.

The best thing a novice marbler can do is make up their own dispersant from dishwashing liquid, and this is what I use for all my classes. It's cheaper and it smells much better! The dishwashing liquid must be heavily diluted with water first. It's hard to give an exact recipe for this since all detergents have different strengths, but a starting point of 1 teaspoon of detergent to 1 cup of water will give you a good baseline. If you find you are having to add a lot of it to make your paint spread, you can make a more concentrated version simply by adding more detergent to the mix. I tend to make up a batch and keep it in a large bottle, then decant a small amount into a container ready for each session.

Glass bottles containing ox gall and dilute detergent.

Mixing step by step:

1. Start by adding a small amount of paint to a clean container. Around a heaped teaspoon (a US ounce) will do.

2. Next, add water to thin the paint. Use a pipette or small spoon to add small amounts until the paint is the consistency of thin olive oil—slightly thicker than milk but not as gloopy as oil. For the dairy-intolerant, I find the consistency to be more like cashew or hazelnut milk than rice milk!

3. Mix the paint and water gently until fully combined. Some paints like to be thinner than others. This base recipe can be adjusted and is a good starting point for a bit of trial and error.

4. Add a single drop of dispersant and stir gently to avoid creating bubbles. This will allow the paint to break the surface tension of the *size* and spread—instead of balling up and sinking.

Now to test the paint! It is best to do this on a smaller test tray of *size* that is the same thickness and temperature as the *size* in your actual tray. Before applying the paint, it's important to skim the *size* in your tray (see page 34).

5. Applying paint to the test tray can be done in different ways (brushes, pipettes, whisks, etc). Whichever way you choose, it is important not to overload your chosen applicator with too much color. Thinned paint can be very heavy if dropped in large quantities and will have trouble spreading before most of it sinks to the bottom of the tray. Make sure to remove any excess paint on the side of the container before application. If you are using an eyedropper, you may have to use much more dispersant since the droplets of color landing on the *size* will be larger and heavier than those falling from a brush or whisk. The brush is held fairly high above the tray and is tapped gently to produce droplets of paint. These fall to the surface and should spread out across the *size* fairly quickly. It is important that your paints are not too thick on the surface of the *size* at this point. When you start adding more color, the colors you've already laid down get pushed into concentration (that is, become brighter, more opaque, and thicker on the surface). If the paint is too heavy at this stage, any following colors will have trouble spreading and may sink. Also, your paper can hold only so much pigment—if the colors are too thick, they will simply run off the paper. A pale, translucent color like this will still produce a bright impression on the paper due to the high pigment content of the paint. It will get brighter still as more colors are added.

A NOTE ON MIXING METALLICS

Most gouache ranges have a few metallics. These can behave in wildly different ways depending on the brand, and even from color to color within the same brand. It is best to mix a metallic slightly thicker to start with, and to control the spread as much as possible. You want the individual metallic pigment particles to remain as close and as concentrated as possible so they print as bright as possible. The more it is diluted, the farther the particles are spread apart, and you will end up with a very pale, mildly glittery effect.

However, if you can't control the spread with careful mixing, the next best thing is to control it with other paints. Choose a pattern where your metallics will be forced into veins, or use them with other aggressively spreading paints (see the "Patternmaking" section, page 136). There is also an option to use an acrylic metallic with your gouache paints. This is not something I do, but other marblers use them to good effect.

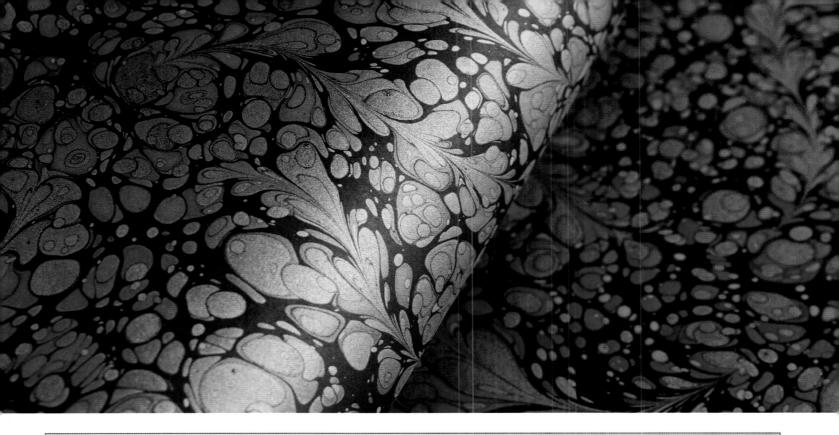

Troubleshooting—Mixing Gouache and Watercolor Paint

Paint is sinking / not spreading: If your paint isn't spreading, first check your *size*—is it the right consistency? Is it too cold? It should be room temperature and the thickness of thin olive oil. Try skimming again and throwing the color seconds afterward. Once you are happy that your *size* is fine, you can adjust your paint. Add water and dispersant, drop by drop, until you have achieved a balanced color. If you are having to add more than a few drops of dispersant, chances are your paint is too thick. Add a little more water and try again. Remember, every time you add water, you are diluting the dispersant— so you may need to add a little of both.

Paint is spreading everywhere and taking over the tray, or it spreads so much it is invisible: you may have overdone it on the dispersant! The only thing to be done is to add more paint to dilute the agent, or to start again. Some paints will spread aggressively on their own without help from a dispersant, due to the makeup of their binders. Watercolors can be especially guilty of this. It is possible to balance your other paints to "fight" this aggression, or to apply the paint at a different point in the pattern with a very dry brush to reduce the amount of paint falling on the surface. Some very interesting patterns and effects can be achieved with unruly paints. However, sometimes you just come across a bad egg, and these few paints are the ones that are better off abandoned and substituted with another brand.

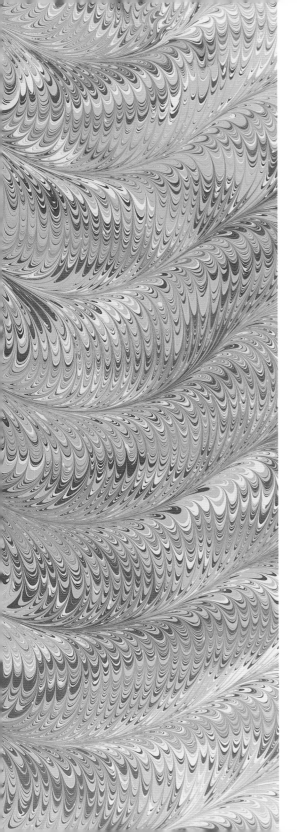

ACRYLIC
MARBLING

Marbling with acrylics is fascinating both for the beginner and the seasoned marbler. For a beginner, they are quick to mix and can produce some wonderful and experimental shapes and colors. For a marbler with experience, the challenge of making them behave the way you want them to is exciting and satisfying—in between the inevitable hair-tearing episodes!

Acrylic paints are a fairly modern medium, having been invented in the mid-twentieth century, and they are extremely popular with contemporary marblers for several good reasons. First, an acrylic paint is water based rather than oil based, making it easy to thin down with water. Second, since they are made with a polymer emulsion, it means that when the water in the paint evaporates, what is left is a flexible, waterproof finish. Materials marbled with acrylics need little or no coating afterward since they are strong and resilient. They are also particularly vibrant when mixed correctly and evenly balanced in the tray.

There are many different brands of acrylics to choose from. Thinly textured "soft"-body or fluid acrylics seem to be the easiest to work with, but the thicker, heavy-body acrylics can also be made to behave when properly mixed with the right amount of water and dispersant. Some good brands to start with are Liquitex Basics, Winsor & Newton Galeria, and Daler Rowney System 3 acrylics. All these come in a wide range of colors, including metallics.

Acrylic colors are easily mixed to create a range of hues. However, as a beginner it is always best to start using colors straight from the tube so you know how they behave separately, before mixing their properties in a new color.

An important thing to consider when using acrylics is what *size* you will use to marble on—they are great in that they can be used with both a carrageenan and a methocel *size*.

Some marblers claim that the former gives them the most control over their paints, but that the acrylics will make the carrageenan spoil quickly. A methocel *size* will keep longer and spoil less quickly; however, it can be harder to make the paints work well and spread evenly. Whichever you decide to use, it's important to keep notes of what works and what doesn't!

MIXING ACRYLIC PAINT FOR MARBLING

What you will need:

- Dispersant—Kodak Photo Flo
- Paint
- *Size*—carrageenan or methocel
- Water—soft or distilled

When mixing acrylics, you will need water (preferably distilled or, at the very least, soft water) and a dispersant. The difficulty with acrylics is that often by their very makeup, they will spread a lot straight from the bottle without any addition of dispersant. This means it can be hard to tell which will fit your requirements without first trying them out. Some acrylics will dominate so much straight out of the tube that it is difficult to make any other paints work with them, and if you are looking for controlled results, then a great deal of testing and tweaking is involved.

Others will need some help dispersing, especially if you have a base color that is aggressively spreading to start with. The best thing to use in this case is something like Kodak Photo Flo, which is a photographic wetting agent. This works far better than ox gall or detergent, both of which are better suited to watercolor and gouache marbling. Acrylic paint will require different levels of water and dispersant, depending on the pigment and the brand. Some acrylic paints are thicker than others and will need more thinning with water. Often a good starting point is to aim for a consistency of thin olive oil—slightly thicker than milk but not as gloopy as oil.

Mixing step by step:

1. Add a small amount of acrylic paint to a clean container.

2. Add water to thin the paint to the consistency of thin olive oil.

3. Mix the paint gently until fully combined. All paints require a differing amount of water, but this is a good starting point for acrylics.

4. It is best to test acrylic paints before adding any dispersant. Do this on a smaller test tray of *size* that is the same consistency and temperature as the *size* in your regular tray. Using a pipette or eyedropper, apply a single drop of paint to the surface of the *size* (remember to skim well first). Adjust the paint if needed. If the paint is sinking below the surface, add dispersant (Photo Flo) one drop at a time, and repeat the single drop of paint to the surface until your paint is floating and spreading well. If a paint is spreading too aggressively straight away, add a little more water—this has the effect of diluting whatever is in the paint that is making it spread too much. With some paints this will give the effect of watering down the color too, so it becomes paler. This problem can be rectified by using other paints to push it back into a higher concentration.

5. It is often a good idea with acrylics to test the paints all together first to see how they behave. You can do this by using a pipette or eyedropper to drop the first color and let it spread into a circle. Then drop another single drop of the next color into the center of the circle, and so on, until you have added a drop each of all your desired colors. You will notice a difference in the thickness of the bands of color. Those with the thinnest bands will often need more dispersant to help them push against those that are spreading more aggressively. You can also test your colors by sprinkling them one by one onto the surface of the test bath. You may want to do this in several different combinations to see how each paint reacts in a different order.

Troubleshooting—Mixing Acrylic Paint

Paint is sinking / not spreading: If your paint is sinking, first check your *size*—is it the right consistency? It should be room temperature and the consistency of thin olive oil. Once you are happy that your *size* is fine, you can adjust your paint. If it is sinking, it is too heavy. You will need to balance it by adding water, dispersant, or both. Start by thinning with a little more water. If this doesn't solve the issue, add dispersant a drop at a time until a single drop of paint spreads without any of it sinking. If your paint is floating but the drops aren't large enough, add dispersant drop by drop until the right-sized circle of paint is achieved.

Paint is spreading everywhere and taking over the tray, or spreads so much it is invisible: Some acrylics will do this automatically because of what they are made of. You can try to work with it and add more dispersant to other colors to "fight" with this color, or accept that this particular paint just behaves this way. You can use its effects to create unusual patterns, or you can abandon it and try another brand—sometimes it is better to just try something new!

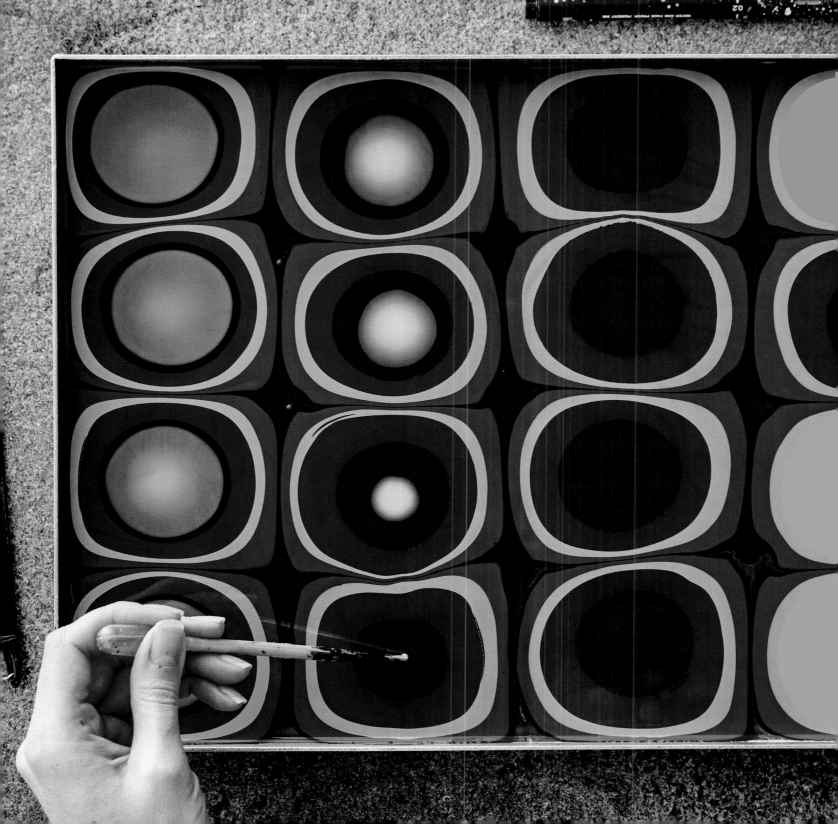

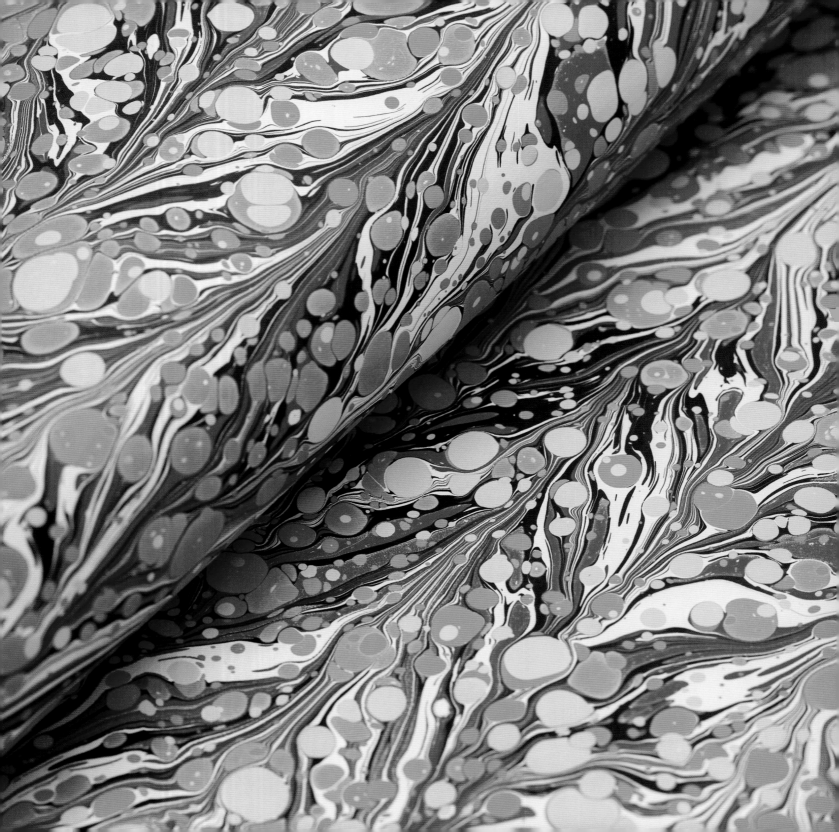

COLOR AND INSPIRATION

INSPIRATION

It's a running joke throughout my classes that I say every part of the marbling process is "my favorite bit about marbling." In some ways, it's true. I do get excited about it, and I can fall in love with any bit of it I choose. I love the way the alummed paper comes out of the pressing boards completely flat. I can't get enough of trying out new paper samples. I find the behavior of different types of paints on the *size* fascinating. The way pigment looks piled up on a palette knife before making it into paint is inexplicably gorgeous to me. I even love when things don't work the way I want them to, because it means I get to indulge the perfectionist in me and keep trying until I get the problem solved (days away from the tray and chocolate help with this!).

You might understand where I'm coming from, or you might think I'm just a bit of a head case. But there's one thing I hope we can agree on—that the best thing about marbling is color! I can't believe you would have picked up this book without being a little bit crazy about it already. In this chapter I hope to encourage you in this love of color (maybe even turn it into an obsession) and give you some practical suggestions on how to go about finding ideas for your own marbled creations, or even other art projects and processes you might have on the go. That's the great thing about inspiration and collecting ideas—you never know what you might end up using them for.

COLLECTING IDEAS

You may be the kind of person who picks up inspiration from everywhere—I am definitely one of those people. Everywhere I go and everything I do is an excuse to pick up ideas. I take pictures, buy postcards, rip pages out of magazines. I make what I laughingly call mood boards, but really they are just collections of things I like that sort of go together for me. I amass color palettes from online designers and paint makers, and I absolutely love Pantone® cards and paint color swatches.

If this isn't you already, I'd like to encourage you to start an ideas sketchbook or just a folder where you keep things you like. It doesn't even have to be physical—keep a folder on your laptop or make use of the incredible resource that is Pinterest. Just start collecting.

The most important task is to craft a collection that moves you in some way. You don't even have to understand how. Pick things that you are drawn to. It might be that you love the color or texture of something. An image might make you feel calm, or invigorated, or even hungry. Take photos of things, keep a piece of that fabric you found in a thrift store, buy a postcard of that painting you stood in front of for ages at the gallery. I even keep things that I'm not sure of, because even if I don't like it, it has produced a reaction in me, and tastes do change—one day I might love it.

The idea behind collecting this variety is to feed your creativity. I often see it as a compost heap of thoughts and images that swirl around together, changing and combining, and becoming fertile ground for any ideas that happen to plant themselves in my mind. However you see it, it is a process of input and output—you have to put interesting things in, to get something creative out.

Keeping a sketchbook and collecting things such as postcard artworks can inspire new color palettes.

Textures and objects can also be interesting sources of inspiration; the patina on this tiny tray shows a multitude of colors.

WHERE TO FIND IDEAS

If I'm feeling a bit bored of my collections or need a bit of an inspiration kick start, here are some places I go and things I do:

• Libraries and bookstores

I adore libraries. They are a happy place for me. I've been a regular library goer since I was a kid, and I still get the same feeling about them—that they are somehow limitless and timeless. Bookstores, on the other hand, feel fresh, with new books constantly coming out, and always something new to discover. I have a habit of deliberately seeking out books that have nothing to do with my usual interests. You can find me rifling through books on architecture, fashion, eighteenth-century pottery design: it doesn't really matter to me. I'm convinced that whatever I take in can at some point inform my practice.

Here's an odd example for you. I still remember a Victorian book I stumbled across at university about planting a garden orchard. The names of the apple and pear varieties were gorgeous, and the careful drawings of the leaves and fruits were fine and beautiful. But I loved it mostly for its words. Years later, while looking at the colors in a picture of a peach tree, I suddenly remembered that book and knew I wanted to create some delicate, organic patterns based around the colors of leaves and growing fruits. You can see some of the samples here (*right*). My favorite has to be the one on the Japanese paper with the visible fibers. I deliberately chose the paper to add to the natural, organic feel of the pattern. And it doesn't matter that people looking at it won't think "Victorian garden orchard" or even know that I was thinking about mottled leaves or delicate blossoms. But I value those things as having been integral to its creation, and my experience of creation is all the richer for it.

• Galleries and museums

There's an amazing book called *The Artist's Way* by Julia Cameron, in which she encourages the use of regular "artists dates" with yourself, to make you get out of your comfort zone and make time to go and feed your creative consciousness. Galleries and museums are great places to go and do this.

Color and pattern have been used in so many different ways throughout history, by thousands of artists and designers, that there is always something to learn or feel inspired by. Try going somewhere you wouldn't usually go. If you are a regular at galleries full of modern art, head to a museum and look at nineteenth-century kimonos, or for a real change of pace, go to a science exhibition. If art imitates life, go and examine life!

• **Music**

You might be one of those people lucky enough to experience color when listening to music. Even if you aren't, most people associate music with memories or images, or even moods. A good exercise is to put on a piece of music and, while listening, begin to list memories, words, and images that come to mind. You might find some words are already colors, but if not, concentrate on one image or memory. Get a notebook and write about it in terms of the colors you see in it. What are they? What feel do the colors give the image? Are they bright or muted? Are there lots of different colors or different tints and shades of the same color?

The other great thing about using music as a springboard is the art that often accompanies it. Vinyl album art is almost a genre in itself. I find myself looking at the colors and shapes on album covers. Sometimes it seems right and fits the music; sometimes it doesn't. Sometimes the music can shift my mood and feelings about a color. Either way, the combining of these two forms is always an enjoyable way to get myself feeling fired up about getting creative.

• **Fairs and shows and looking at others' work**

One of the best places for inspiration is looking at the work of other artists. For me, this could mean visiting an interior-design or craft fair. Often other people will fuse together elements that hadn't occurred to you, or have used two colors together you usually hate, but made them really work.

The other place to look is, of course, at the work of other marblers, both historical and current. There are so many historical examples of marbling: online, in books, and in libraries. It's worth exploring to see where the art has been in order to build on it. It is most definitely worth searching out contemporary marblers and their work to see what can be achieved—it's all so inspiring.

I am very keen to stress here that I don't mean you to copy their work: admire it and appreciate their hard-earned skill, and let it feed your ideas. I've included in this book a section on marbling artists I personally admire (see pages 172–175), but it is in no way an exhaustive list. There are many talented marblers in the world, and their number is only growing— perhaps you will become one of them. Take these as a starting point and then go out there and search for more.

• **Taking a walk**

This may seem overly simple. Perhaps it is, but color combinations are everywhere. The next page shows an exercise to help you train yourself to spot them more easily.

TRAIN YOUR EYE

This is one of my favorite practical ways of teaching students to be responsive to sources of inspiration. For the purposes of marbling, I've concentrated here mainly on color. This exercise can be used in specific places and scenarios such as those I've just discussed, or just to be more consciously and subconsciously receptive in daily life. This method is a great way to concentrate your eye and seek out color (or shape or pattern, etc.). And you can be as general or as specific as you like and find.

I love to take photos of interesting colors and shapes I see when out and about, to add to my ideas bank.

1. Start by choosing something you want to be more receptive to: this should be fairly specific. It could be a particular color (such as red), or a shape (such as circles), or something else, such as texture, shadow, or straight lines.

2. Go for a walk—give yourself a fighting chance—don't choose the color fuchsia and then go walking in the woods in winter. You are going to be disappointed! As you go, make a conscious effort to look around you and seek out the thing you have chosen to see more of. If it is a color, make a mental note (or a real one in a notebook, or even take a photo) every time you see that color. If you have chosen a shape, do the same every time you see the shape.

3. Whatever you see, really notice what it is. If it's a color you're looking for, notice what other colors are around it. Consider the exercise as simply or as elaborately as you like. If you're looking for color, here are some questions to ask yourself to get more from the exercise:

   • What is the object? What is its purpose? How does the color relate to the form?
   • Is it a dominant color or a small part of a larger palette?
   • Is it bright or muted?
   • Is it a block color or does it have different tones and shades?
   • Is it a pure color? For example, if it's blue, is it a green blue or a red blue?
   • What kind of light is falling on it? How does this impact the color and its effect?
   • Is it particularly effective or eye-catching? Is it pleasing?
   • How do you personally respond to it?
   • If you are working on something in particular, could you use this somehow in what you are working on?
   • Does it spark any immediate thoughts or images?

4. Then add your notes to an ideas sketchbook or moodboard. I like to do this most when I've been given a specific brief around a color, or when I know I am going to be working with a color I'm not too fond of. It can be interesting to do this while walking around—what kinds of reds do you find in a supermarket compared to, say, a fancy gift store? You can do this anywhere, even for five minutes while you are waiting to meet someone for coffee.

After deciding once to seek out the color pink, I made notes in a book that described a woman's pink skirt and green boots as she sat at a bus stop, from my position on the top deck of a London bus. You don't even need to leave home—take yourself on a virtual wander around images on the internet or in a book. It really can be done anywhere.

Keep a notebook describing the behavioral properties of your paints, and later on your recipes.

COLOR

CHOOSING COLORS AND COLOR PALETTES
Inspiration and collecting color ideas are one thing, but applying them to the process of marbling is quite another. I know what you really want to do is skip this and just get on with the "how to" bit—and you should! Do you think that when I first started to learn to marble that first I went to my sketchbook of ideas and thought about color palettes or what pigments are made of? Well, I didn't. I took my (extremely basic) skills and *The Whole Art of Marbling* by Charles Woolnough from 1853, and I set up my tray next to my kitchen sink and got on with doing it. And that was important. I spent a good few years at that sink learning about my materials, and it was there that I realized the need to record what I was seeing in the tray.

WORKING FROM THE TUBE
Marbling can be a wild business at first. Getting the *size* right, coating the paper properly, making sure you have all your materials at the same temperature—it's a lot to think about. In a way, as a beginner, complex palettes and color mixing should be the last thing on your list. As mentioned before, I always encourage my novice students to start with colors straight out of the paint tubes, because of the different way each pigment behaves. This way, you can really get a handle on the properties of each color before you begin mixing and adding their properties together.

It is really important to make notes on each color too. Looking back over my old notebooks, I have scrawled next to paint names observations that just read, "Why? Why is it doing this?" and "Aggressive. Really aggressive." Once you've sorted out how your tube colors are working, you are in a great position to start mixing. Got a color that is really pale and transparent?

Mix it with a bit of an opaque color to give it body. That red that always sinks? Add a touch of the orange that wants to flash from one end of the tray to the other. The more you know your paint, the more control you will have.

COLOR MIXING

Before beginning to mix colors, it is worth having a basic knowledge of color theory. It is a vast subject that has been developed and discussed for centuries, with many writers and artists developing principles on the use and effect of color. From how to put colors together to evoking mood and emotion with different hues, to the cultural and social influences of color, there's a lot of information out there. You may be aware of some of the basic theory already, as well as perhaps being familiar with the color wheel. It's a great tool to refer back to when building your color palettes.

Let's cover the basics of color mixing. This three-part color wheel (below) is split into primary, secondary, and tertiary colors.

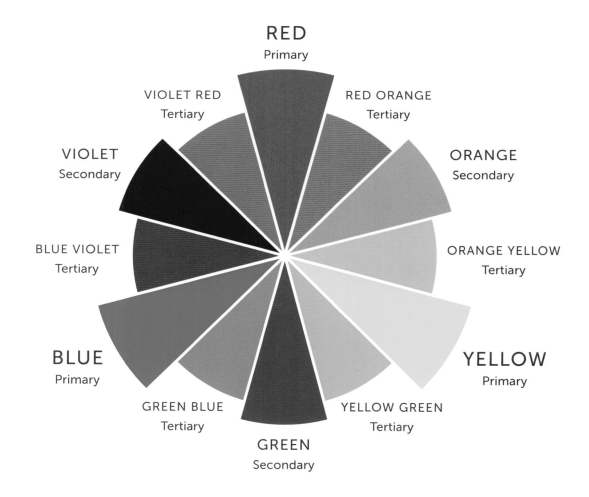

• **Primary colors**—Red, yellow, and blue. In traditional color theory, these three colors cannot be made by mixing any other colors. All other colors are made from combinations of these three hues.

• **Secondary colors**—Orange, green, violet. These colors are made by mixing two of the primary colors together.

• **Tertiary colors**—Red orange, yellow orange, yellow green, blue green, blue violet, red violet. These colors are made by mixing a primary and a secondary color.

By using the information in the color wheel, you can easily mix a whole range of colors from a few basic tubes of paint. If you want to make brown, try mixing equal amounts of a color with its complement. The colors on the wheel assume a ratio of 1:1 of each mixing color used, but by adjusting the ratio, you can produce many, many more.

Creating Color Palettes

The color wheel is a great guide for creating color combinations with visual harmony. These are a few basic formulas for you to try as a starting point.

• **Analogous colors**—These are three colors that sit next to each other on the color wheel. For example, green, yellow green, and yellow.

• **Complementary colors**—These are combinations of colors that are opposite each other on the color wheel; for example, orange and blue.

• **Triadic colors**—These are three colors equally spaced apart on the color wheel. For example, orange, green, and violet.

• **Split complementary**—A color and the two colors either side of its complement. For example, violet, yellow green, and yellow orange.

• **Monochromatic**—concentrating on using just one color, but varying its value (see what I mean on the next page).

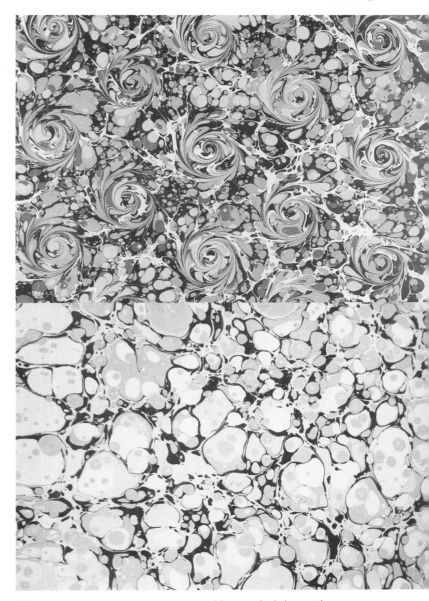

Although both these schemes have blue as their base, they are very different. The first is a bright and vibrant palette made with tints of the base blue, plus the contrasting addition of its complement, orange. The second image uses tones of blue for a muted, more traditional stone pattern.

You can expand the range of colors in your palette really easily by adjusting the value (lightness or darkness) of one or more of your hues by adding black and white. Doing this creates tints and shades, as shown below.

You can also adjust a color's saturation (purity or brilliance) by adding gray—these are called tones. This results in more-muted colors. You can also change the saturation by adding a little of the color's complement; for example, adding a touch of orange to blue. These adjustments can add depth and interest to even the very simplest color schemes.

• Tints are created by adding white to a base hue.
• Shades are made by adding black.
• Tones are made by adding gray (a bit of tinting and shading).

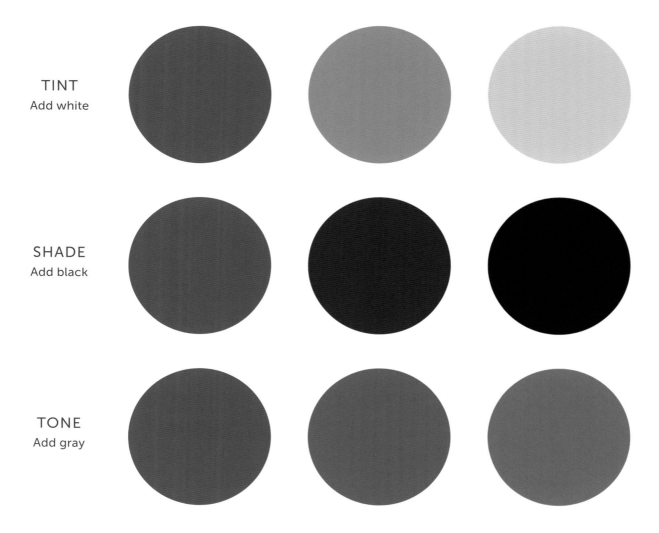

TINT
Add white

SHADE
Add black

TONE
Add gray

Using Pictures and Objects to Design a Color Palette

Pictures in magazines and books, or patterns on fabrics and papers, will often contain excellent examples of colors that work together. Take a look through your inspiration collection and pick out an image or object whose colors you like. Notice how the designer or photographer has applied some of the color theory principles or maybe played with your expectations about what colors should be together. Try making a couple of schemes of up to five colors each by producing swatches (using the paints you plan to marble with) of colors you pick from the image or object. If you are using an image that has areas of light and shadow, notice how a single color can change in different lights. It may produce a tint, a tone, or a shade—or even a color similar to the original, but with the slight addition of another color.

You might produce a scheme you like, but if you don't, cut up each separate color swatch you've made (label them or make notes on each first, so you can remember how to remake it!) and spend some time moving them around and putting different ones next to each other. Do this a few times with different objects and images, and you'll end up with a great bank of your own color cards that you can mix and match for myriad new combinations, based on the paints you have.

You can also easily create your own color palettes from pictures by using photographic or computer software, or use an app on your phone or laptop. Some software you have to pay for, but there are some excellent free websites and apps that allow you to upload a picture and then pull palettes from the colors in it. Many will let you adjust colors and the amount of saturation too, so you can tweak the tones to your heart's content. Many of these can be exported and used to inspire your paint mixing. A lot of websites will also let you save and share your color schemes and,

Making paint swatches and building palettes from pictures.

Turning a palette into a marbled test print and pairing it with materials for bookbinding.

Look at how these photographs inspire different color palettes. Try the same exercise with your pictures and photos.

furthermore, give you access to huge libraries of user-created palettes.

All of this is just the tip of the color iceberg. As you will find in the next section of the book, there are so many marbled

patterns you can make, that even one color palette can create a huge range of different effects. The examples (*opposite*) show just one color palette that's been mixed around and used with different patterns and different-colored papers.

PATTERNMAKING

BEGINNING TO MARBLE

The *size* is ready, the paint is prepped, and you can skim like a pro—so it's time to make some patterns!

The following pages take you step by step through twenty-six different patterns, but this is by no means an exhaustive list. There are hundreds of different patterns, some traditional, some contemporary, but the selection here offers a solid base for you to experiment with and build on.

All the patterns in this section are created with gouache and watercolor and fall into four broad categories. To some extent, they increase in difficulty as you progress through them. These categories are

• **Stone and Gelgit patterns**

• **Nonpareil patterns**

• **Chevron patterns**

• **Other patterns**

Once you become familiar with how they are made, you will find that often you can analyze a pattern that you have found elsewhere and work out how it was done. Sometimes in the process of working out a pattern, you accidentally end up making another one. Just be sure to keep notes on whatever you do!

Recording is the first step to understanding and replicating (or avoiding!) the results of your early experiments—because that is what they will be to start with. However much I'd like marbling to be an exact science, there is still an amount of trial and error, even for those of us who are marbling regularly or in a professional capacity. But the experiments are fun. Go into patternmaking with an open attitude and you won't be disappointed. Be amazed and curious about your results. Find it magical—it is!—and make peace and come to terms with the fact that there will be (many) frustrations.

This book is designed to kick-start your marbling journey. You will produce something with the instructions in this book, and every sheet is an experience. It might not be as you imagined or even hoped, but every marble is another lesson. So here's an expression I drag out in pretty much every class I teach, which is trite but true: there are no mistakes, just experiences.

APPLYING COLORS TO THE BATH

Brush

Every time you go to use any paint, it is always best to give it a gentle stir before using it to make sure everything is well mixed. If you are using a brush, you will want to hold it about 12 in. above the tray—this will give you a more even spread of color. You can either tap the brush on your finger or onto a stick, or tap the top of your brush. I find this works best for me since it encourages most of the paint to fall down toward the bath and not bounce upward. Different bristles will make one

method easier than another. The closer to the bath you get, the smaller the area the paint drops will cover, and the more directional your drops will be.

Whisk

Whisks work best when tapped against a stick or rod to encourage the drops of paint to fall onto the *size*. In general, the drier the whisk, the smaller the drops of paint. The amount of paint you need to use with a whisk will also depend on what it is made of. Try to remove some of the excess paint on the side of the pot before beginning. You can see examples of whisks being used in the "Fabric Marbling" section on page 159.

Eyedropper/Pipette

When using an eyedropper or pipette, it is important to make sure you have mixed your paints so that the heavy drop quickly disperses across the surface of the *size* without sinking. To help it, you can also hold your eyedropper or pipette close to the surface when you release the paint. Don't forget to maintain pressure on the bulb of the dropper once you have begun—releasing it just a bit will pull air back into the dropper and give you bubbles on your *size* when you drop more paint. You can drop in a random fashion, or in a more regimented "bull's-eye" pattern. You can see this in more depth in the "Fabric Marbling" section from page 148 onward.

USING METALLICS

There are many examples of marblers using metallic paints in their work, and their success lies in knowing how each particular paint behaves. To ensure a bright, iridescent effect, they need to be controlled in certain ways to maintain a high concentration of pigment. When choosing a pattern, look for one where the paint can be pushed into concentration, and use it first so it can be made into tight veins, or use it at the end over another aggressive paint so it can't spread too thinly. As with all other paints, the key is balance, and using the behavioral properties to your advantage.

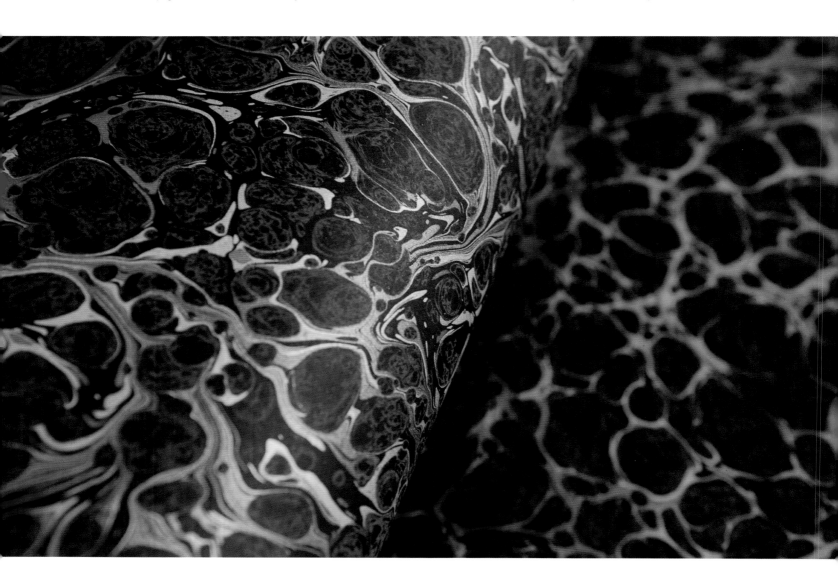

LAYING THE PAPER

Once you have made your pattern, you are going to want to get that paper down before the paint starts to dry or break up. Grab a sheet, and check which side is the back (remember the pencil mark) and which side is alum coated. You really don't want to get this wrong. In the words of Charles Woolnough, watching your paint run off an unalummed sheet will cause you "indescribable annoyance and vexation."

Take the paper in both hands and hold as little of it as possible at opposite corners. Lay one corner down onto the bath—but don't let it go—with a smooth, fluid movement, then gently lower the rest of the paper down onto the surface of the *size*. This method is the least likely to catch air bubbles or create odd lines on your paper. Before lifting the paper off the *size*, give it a gentle tap all over. This will help shift any cheeky air bubbles that may be hiding under there. Once the paper has made contact with the surface of the *size*, the pattern can't be changed by movement. You can even lift and drop the paper back down and it would not pick up any more paint.

Sometimes you'll find that your papers begin to curl when you are putting them down onto the *size*. This is completely normal, and some papers are more prone to do it than others. What happens is that paper fibers expand when wet and contract when dry. The side of the paper hitting the *size* expands while the back of the paper remains dry, and the curling occurs due to the differing tensions on both sides of the paper. There are ways around this, such as making sure you are using your papers just as they have stopped being damp, or misting them with water on the back before laying them down. But often the best thing is to simply lay your paper smoothly and promptly once it is out of the boards. If it starts to curl after it has been laid on the bath, remove it and be sure to rinse both sides of the paper. Wetting both sides should bring the paper out of the curl.

RINSING THE PAPER

To remove the paper, gently peel it back off the surface of the *size* over a dowel or rod, or pull it onto a flat wooden or metal rinsing board. It's a good idea to set up a rinsing station at a sink or over another tray nearby.

If you are using a dowel or rod, your rinsing can be as simple as holding the draped paper under a gently running tap. If you are using a board, you will want to prop it up either in a sink or in another tray and use a jug or hose attachment to rinse over your paper.

The key is to rinse gently, since the paint will not be fully fixed on the paper until it is dry. Once they're rinsed, either hang your papers with pegs from a line, hang over an airer, or leave flat to air-dry. Marbled papers must be completely dry before stacking.

FLATTENING THE PAPER

You will probably find that your paper has curled while drying (another wet/dry paper fiber phenomenon), and this is completely normal. The easiest and safest way to flatten them is to stack them under a heavy flat board with lots of weight on top until the papers have relaxed and flattened. The amount of time this takes will depend on paper type. You can iron your papers too, but be careful to do so from the back of the paper with an iron that is not too hot. It is always good practice to use another piece of paper or greaseproof paper to protect it while ironing, to reduce the risk of scorch.

EVALUATING PATTERNS

As a beginner, the most important thing is to just play and learn about your materials. As you come to grow in skill as a marbler, you will begin to get a sense of creating work that has deliberate composition. Experimenting is key here, and it can be helpful to have an idea of the print's final purpose.

Will your paper cover a box or a book? Will it be an art piece? How large will it be? Is it important to be able to see very clear, fine detail, or will it need to make a big impact from far away?

The tendency as a novice marbler is to go too far. It's always tempting to go in with one more color. "One more swirl" is often the precursor to "muddy swamp." While these experiments are an excellent learning curve for the beginner, as you begin to improve it is worth employing a little restraint. Resist that last pass with the stylus; put down that seventh color!

It is a good idea to critically appraise your own work. Ask yourself what makes it successful or unsuccessful. This will, of course, mean different things to different people and will depend on the final use of the piece, but here are some questions you could usefully ask:

- How does your eye travel over the print? Does it catch on a certain color, or trip over a bunch of large stones that happened when you overloaded your brush?

- Is the pattern balanced and even? Does it need to be?

- Does it need an element of "lift" in the form of a tint or a saturated color?

- Should there be one paint that spreads three times the size of the others? Does it matter?

- Perhaps most importantly—do you like it?

REPEATING PATTERNS

Although every single pattern made is unique, there is something deeply satisfying about being able to create the

"same" paper several times. There is no real secret to repeating the same patterns over and over except to take copious notes and practice, practice, practice!

I have learned never to throw away a marble pattern or experiment unless it truly is beyond saving. I have files and files of tests and samples, and folders of "not-quite-rights." They get added into my inspiration collection in case one day I want to come back to a color palette of pink and green and gray that wasn't at all what I'd planned at the time. I also keep my mistakes to remind me of what not to try again. I try to keep a

swatch of most of the papers I make as a physical record, and they are useful if I ever want or need to re-create them. The whole sheets that haven't quite worked I keep so I can try a bit of overmarbling (see page 134), which can sometimes turn them from "disaster" into "complete success."

BEYOND THE BOOK

The patterns included here are both traditional and contemporary, but all have an element of order. You can play with all these bases to create endless versions, or change it up completely by experimenting. There really are no rules.

Things that you can experiment with:

- **Colors**—Head back to the "Color and Inspiration" section (page 58 onward) for ideas on how to change your color schemes.

- **Paper**—Change the paper type, or the paper color. If your paint is slightly translucent, the paper color will change the hue of the paints on the top. Patterns can take on a different feel when the paper is changed, as in the first image below.

- **Patterns**—Try your less-than-exciting color palette with another pattern. Notice in the second image below how one color palette can have a completely different effect, depending on the pattern you choose to use it on.

- **Size of the paint drops**—Do this by increasing the spread with dispersant, or by creating very tiny dots of color on your marbling bath.

- **Empty space**—Try masking off areas of your paper with low-tack tape and paper shapes before marbling it, or by cutting shapes into some paper and laying it on the bath after you've made your pattern, but before you've laid your paper.

- **Paint additives**—There is most certainly historical precedent for adding interesting substances to paint. Lots of different household chemicals can be used to create all manner of peculiar and wonderful effects. Grab something and try. Got an egg? Chuck in some egg white. I've played with everything I can find in my house and studio for some truly weird and special effects. PVA glue, wheat paste, oils, moisturizer, cleaning products—all these and more have graced my tray. It is always best to try things out at the end of a session, and be ready for some deep cleaning of the tray and tools afterward (lots of hot water or rubbing alcohol, or both, can help remove all remaining residues).

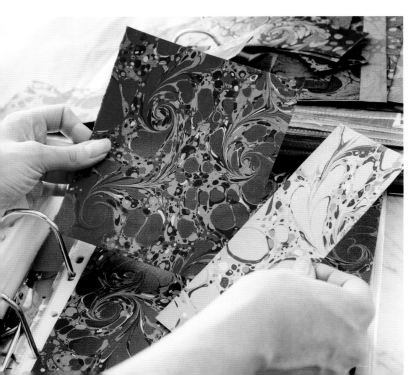

STONE PATTERNS

TURKISH STONE

The oldest and simplest pattern to create, and yet one of the most effective and appealing, is the Turkish Stone. The act of tapping paint onto the marbling bath is called "throwing stones." It is the basis for all marbled patterns, although there are different ways of achieving it. Here you can see it produced with a paintbrush, while later, in the "Fabric Marbling" section, it is made using whisks and eyedroppers. The first color dropped gets pushed into veins by the other colors thrown down after it.

There are no set rules as to what colors should go on first, or how many colors a Turkish Stone should have. This example uses four colors.

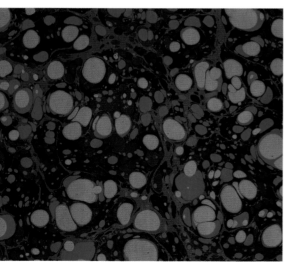

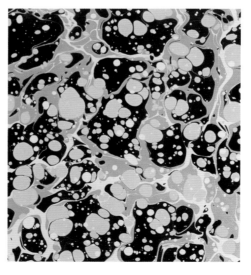

1. Start by gathering your prepared colors and skim your *size* until the surface is clear.

2. Making sure not to overload your brush, apply your first color. The aim is to "flood" the bath or cover the surface quickly and evenly. You don't want a heavy layer, since this color will get the most compressed.

3. Apply your second color—make sure it spreads well. You will notice the first color getting pushed into veins.

4. Apply your subsequent colors.

5. Once you have finished, the first color applied should have become thin veins, and the other colors spread evenly without sinking.

6. Holding your paper alummed side down, lay your paper carefully onto the surface of the bath. Tap to release any air bubbles trapped beneath it.

7. Peel your paper off the marbling bath, either onto a board or over a stick, and rinse gently. Hang up to dry.

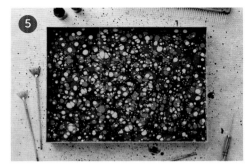

DRAWN STONE OR "FREESTYLE" STONE

This can be a very elegant and organic pattern. Vary the width of your stylus to create different effects—a thicker stylus will create more drag and movement than a thin one.

1. Flood the bath with your first color.

2. Apply all your subsequent colors.

3. Use a stylus to draw randomly over the pattern, either in a single or multiple passes across the stones.

4. Lay the paper, give it a tap, and then peel the paper off the bath. Rinse, then hang up to dry.

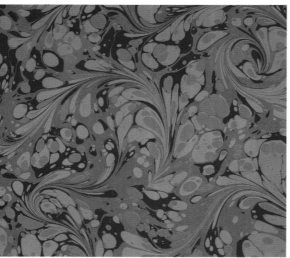

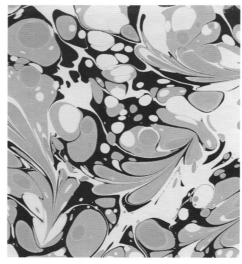

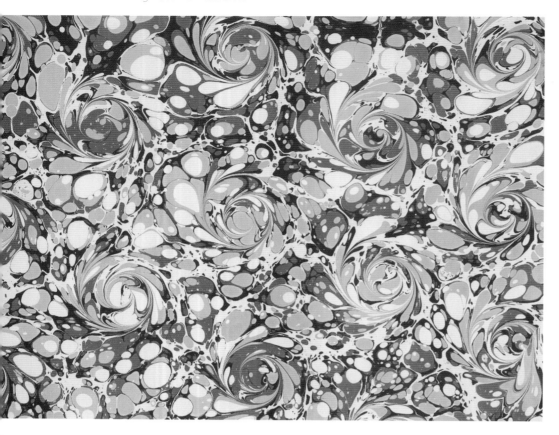

SNAIL PATTERN

This was developed and became popular in the 1600s. You can make this pattern with either a stylus or a bouquet comb (see page 27). Many historical examples show the curls very close or even touching. This example shows a larger space between the curls in a half-drop repeat. Curls of different sizes can have an interesting effect on this pattern, as can the size of the stones.

1. Flood the bath with your first color.

2. Apply all your subsequent colors.

3. Using a bouquet comb or a stylus, draw curls over the stones in a regular, even fashion.

4. Continue until the pattern is complete.

5. Lay the paper, give a gentle tap, and then peel the paper from the bath and rinse gently. Hang up to dry.

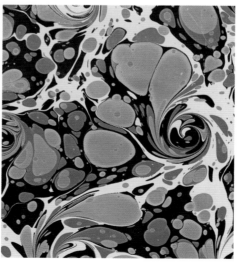

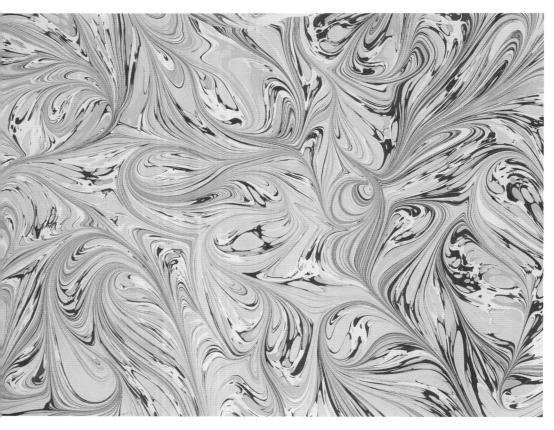

FANTASY PATTERN

What makes this a Fantasy pattern—and not a Drawn Stone—is the fact that by the end, no stones can be seen. Try different thicknesses of stylus to change the appearance of this pattern.

1. Flood the bath with your first color.

2. Apply all your subsequent colors.

3. Use a stylus to draw randomly through the stones so no stones are left anywhere on the tray.

4. Lay your paper, tap, and peel off the bath. Rinse gently. Hang up to dry.

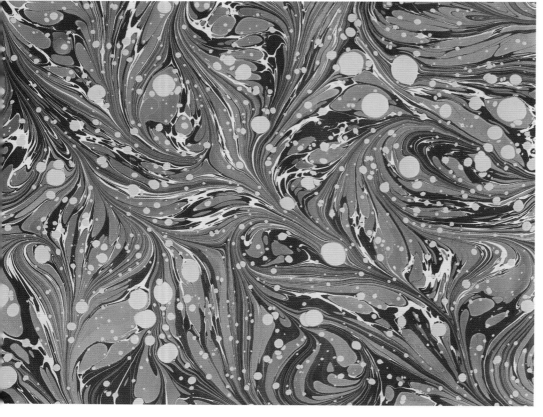

FANTASY PATTERN WITH STONE

A real favorite of mine. Change up the size or number of stones thrown in step 4 to alter the pattern.

1. Flood the bath with your first color.

2. Apply all your subsequent colors.

3. Use a stylus to draw randomly through the stones so no stones are left, as in a Fantasy pattern.

4. Throw a layer of stones over the top of the Fantasy pattern.

5. Lay your paper, tap, and peel off the bath. Rinse gently. Hang up to dry.

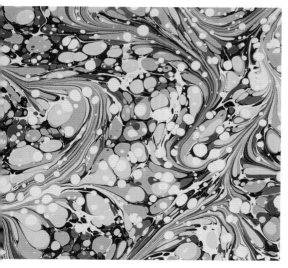

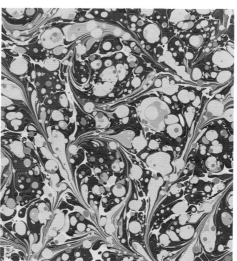

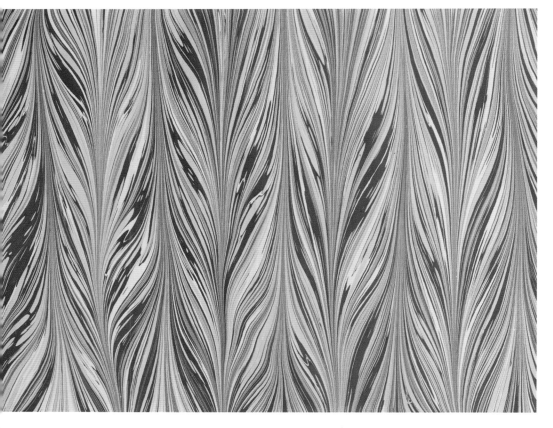

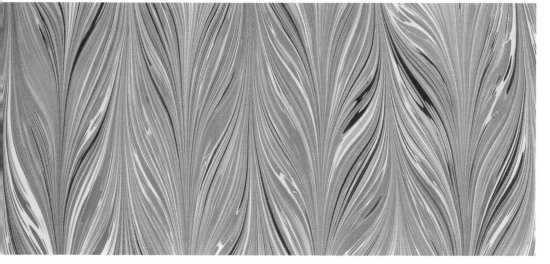

GELGIT PATTERNS

Gelgit is a Turkish word meaning "to come and go," or "ebb and flow." It is very fitting for a pattern in which your tools go back and forth across the bath. You can use either a stylus or a rake for this pattern. The pictures show a stylus, but the rake method is described as well. The speed at which you complete this pattern will have an effect on its outcome, as will the thickness of your stylus (or rake pins). The Gelgit is rarely seen as a pattern on its own but is the base for many other combed patterns.

1. Apply all your colors to the bath.

2. Starting at one corner, draw your stylus horizontally along one edge of the bath to the other corner. Turn and draw the stylus back along the edge of the line you have just drawn. Continue to do this until the tray is covered. The depth of the gap you leave between lines will also affect the appearance of this pattern.

3. Repeat step 2 vertically, so the lines are perpendicular to the first set.

4. Lay your paper, tap, and peel your print from the bath. Rinse gently and hang up to dry.

Directions for using a rake:

If using a rake, choose one with pins between 1 and 2 in. (2.5–5 cm) apart.

- Apply colors. Put the rake in the bath at one end and pull it across to the other side, with one pin running along the edge of the tray.

- At the end, move the rake so the pins are in the middle of the lines you have just made. Push the rake back up the bath to the other end, bisecting these lines.

- Repeat previous step in the opposite direction so the second set of lines is perpendicular to the first.

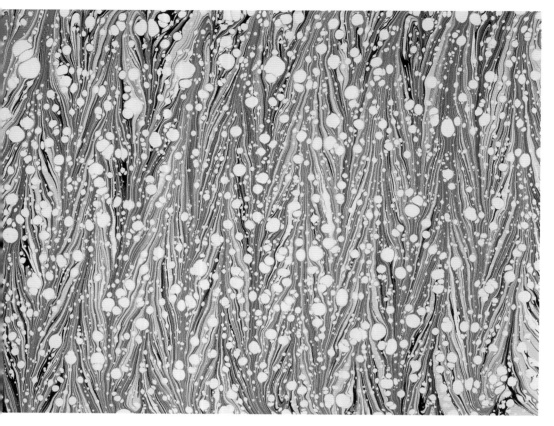

ZEBRA PATTERN

Built on the Gelgit pattern, a Zebra has a final layer of stones laid down at the end. This pattern can be changed by adapting the size of the last stones thrown, or by throwing more than one color at the end.

1. Apply your colors in a Stone pattern.

2. Begin your Gelgit by going back and forth one way.

3. Finish the Gelgit by repeating the back and forth motion in the opposite direction.

4. Throw a final color over the top of the Gelgit. This can be a new color, or one you have already used. A drier brush will give you smaller stones.

5. Lay the paper, tap, and peel from the tray. Rinse gently and hang up to dry.

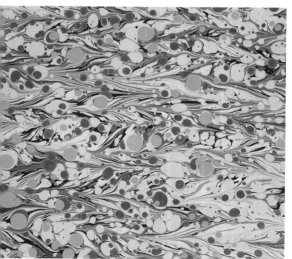

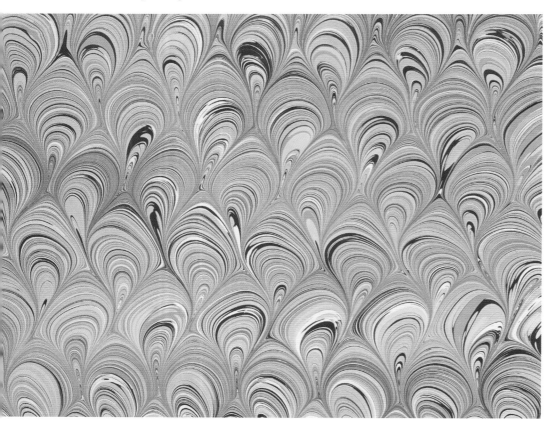

PEACOCK PATTERN

Also known as a Shell pattern, this pattern requires the use of a bouquet comb. It can take a bit of practice to get the movements smooth and consistent across the pattern.

1. Apply your colors in a Stone pattern.

2. Begin your Gelgit by going back and forth one way.

3. Finish the Gelgit by repeating the back-and-forth motion in the opposite direction.

4. Place your bouquet comb to the left side at the top of the tray. Move it down in a gentle wave. The size of the wave movement will depend on the tooth spacing of your comb. You should aim to move your comb no more than the length of the spacing between your pins, both horizontally and vertically, as you make the wave. When creating the peacock, you must move the bouquet comb down the tray in the opposite direction to the last pass of your Gelgit.

5. The aim is to create consistent shapes across your pattern.

6. Lay the paper, tap, and peel from the tray. Rinse gently and hang up to dry.

NONPAREIL PATTERNS

From the French meaning "matchless" or "without equal," the Nonpareil is one of the most transformative patterns of all. Varying the width of the tooth spacing in your comb will produce different effects—the spacing used here is 0.2 in. (0.5 cm). A comb with a tooth spacing wider than 0.4 in. (1 cm) creates a Cascade pattern. You will need to ensure that your comb fits the width of your tray—any shorter and the pattern will warp. The way you make your Gelgit can also affect how this pattern turns out. Try it with a thicker stylus or vary the speed or line spacing.

1. Apply your colors in a Stone pattern.

2. Begin your Gelgit by going back and forth one way.

3. Finish the Gelgit by repeating the back-and-forth motion in the opposite direction.

4. Take your comb and pull it steadily across the tray in the opposite direction to the last pass of your Gelgit. Avoid scraping the bottom of your tray.

5. Lay the paper, tap, and peel from the tray. Rinse gently and hang up to dry.

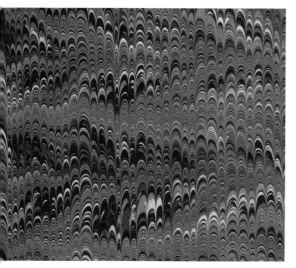

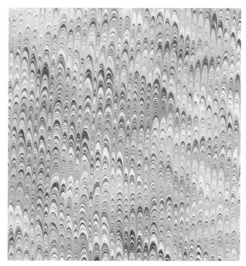

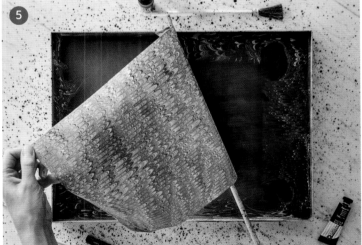

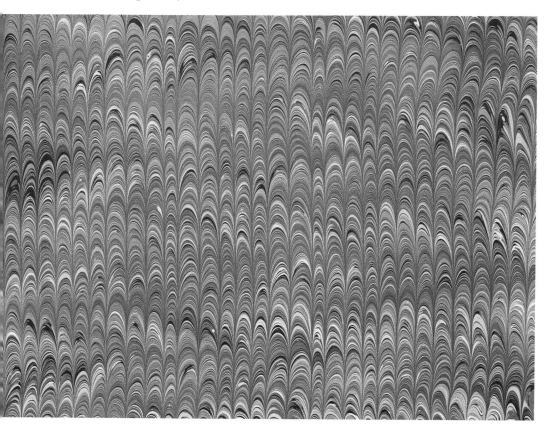

CASCADE

Similar to the Nonpareil, the Cascade pattern is made with a comb that has a tooth spacing of 0.4 in. (1 cm) or larger. Varying the width of the tooth spacing in your comb produces different effects—the spacing used here is 0.4 in. (1 cm). The way you make your Gelgit also affects how this pattern turns out. Try it with a thicker stylus or vary the speed or spacing of the lines.

1. Apply your colors in a Stone pattern.

2. Begin the Gelgit by going back and forth one way.

3. Finish the Gelgit by repeating the back-and-forth motion in the opposite direction.

4. Take your comb and pull it steadily across the tray in the opposite direction to the last pass of your Gelgit. Avoid scraping the bottom of your tray.

5. Lay the paper, tap, and peel from the tray. Rinse gently and hang up to dry.

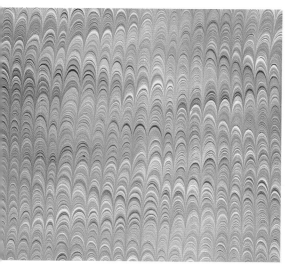

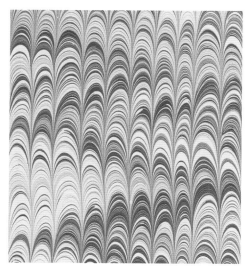

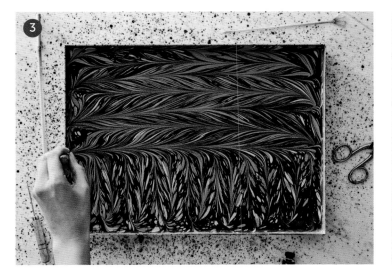

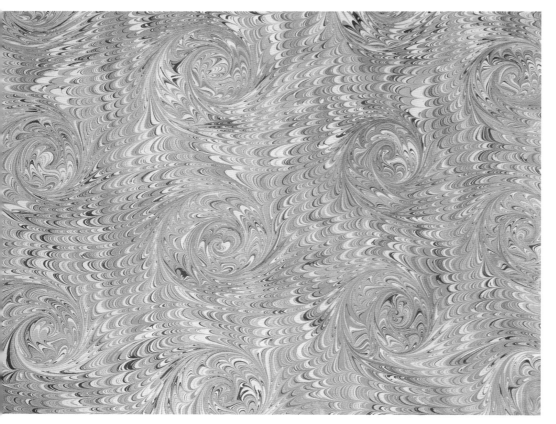

FRENCH CURL

This impressive, historical pattern is made over a Nonpareil. The comb used in this pattern is 0.2 in. (0.5 cm). The curls in this pattern can be made using a rake or a stylus. You can even use a large bouquet comb to help stagger the curls.

1. Apply your colors in a Stone pattern.

2. Begin the Gelgit by going back and forth one way.

3. Finish the Gelgit by repeating the back-and-forth motion in the opposite direction.

4. Take your comb and pull it steadily across the tray in the opposite direction to the last pass of your Gelgit. Avoid scraping the bottom of your tray.

5. Using a rake or a stylus, draw curls evenly across the pattern.

6. Lay the paper, tap, and peel from the tray. Rinse gently and hang up to dry.

ICARUS

The Icarus and Waved Icarus are patterns built on the base of a Nonpareil. This pattern uses a 0.2 in. (0.5 cm) comb and a 1.5 in. (4 cm) rake. This pattern is often seen with the last lines of the rake going horizontally across the pattern, but I love to use the other way as well. Change the pin spacing in your rake for different effects.

1. Apply your colors in a Stone pattern.

2. Begin the Gelgit by going back and forth one way.

3. Finish the Gelgit by repeating the back-and-forth motion in the opposite direction.

4. Create the Nonpareil. Take your comb and pull it steadily across the tray in the opposite direction to the last pass of your Gelgit. Avoid scraping the bottom of your tray.

5. Using a rake, pull across your Nonpareil in the opposite direction to the way you made it, from one edge of the tray to the other.

6. Lay the paper, tap, and peel from the tray. Rinse gently and hang up to dry.

WAVED ICARUS

A slight variation on the Icarus gives this pattern delicacy and movement. This example uses a 0.2 in. (0.5 cm) comb and a 1.5 in. (4 cm) rake. Change the pin spacing in your rake for different effects.

1. Apply your colors in a Stone pattern.

2. Create the Gelgit.

3. Then create the Nonpareil. Take your comb and pull it steadily across the tray in the opposite direction to the last Gelgit pass. Avoid scraping the bottom of your tray.

4. Using a rake, move it in a gentle wave across the Nonpareil in the opposite direction to the way you made it, from one edge of the tray to the other.

5. Lay the paper, tap, and peel from the tray. Rinse gently and hang to up dry.

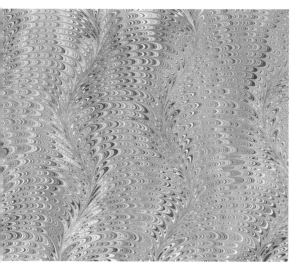

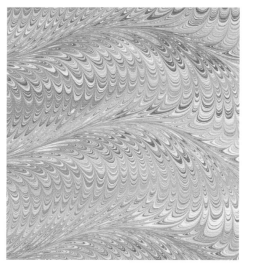

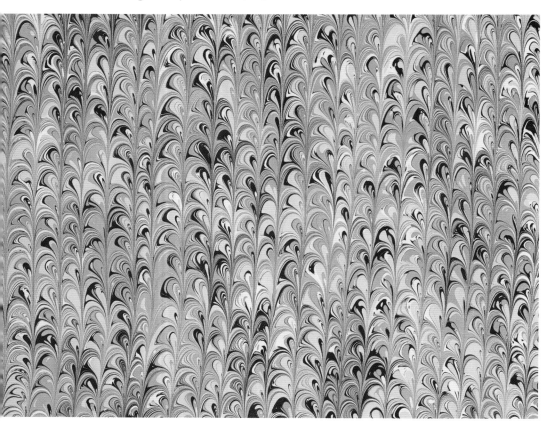

AMERICAN

The American can be an easy pattern to muddy with color, since the bands of paint become very thin and compressed. Here I have chosen to complete half a Gelgit to allow some of the colors to remain in larger quantities. Depending on how you lay down your paint, you may be able to perform a full Gelgit, especially if you are using the eyedropper method. The comb used in this pattern has teeth 0.4 in. (1 cm) apart.

1. Apply the colors in a Stone pattern.

2. Complete a half or full Gelgit.

3. Take the comb and pull it steadily across the tray in the opposite direction to the last pass of your Gelgit.

4. Turn the same comb 90 degrees around, then pull right across the tray from edge to edge.

5. Lay the paper, tap, and peel from the tray. Rinse gently and hang up to dry.

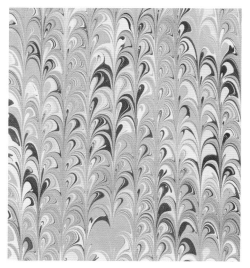

FEATHER

This delicate design is made with different-sized rakes for different effects. Since the paint gets pushed into such fine lines, it is important not to overload your tray with color. Also, make sure your stones are not too small to begin with. The paint drops need a light touch. This pattern is made with a 0.2 in. (0.5 cm) comb and a 1.2 in. (3 cm) rake.

1. Apply your colors in a Stone pattern.

2. Begin your Gelgit by going back and forth one way.

3. Finish the Gelgit by repeating the back-and-forth motion in the opposite direction.

4. Create the Nonpareil. Take your comb and pull it steadily across the tray in the opposite direction to the last pass of your Gelgit. Avoid scraping the bottom of your tray.

5. Using a rake, draw across the tray going in the opposite direction of the Nonpareil.

6. At the bottom of the tray, move the pins of the rake so they are between the lines you have just drawn, and push the rake back across the tray, bisecting them.

7. Lay the paper, tap, and peel from the tray. Rinse gently and hang up to dry.

BOUQUET PATTERN

This pattern uses the bouquet comb and can be hard to master, but it is well worth the time and effort of practice! The example uses a 0.2 in. (0.5 cm) comb and a 1 in. (2.5 cm) bouquet comb.

1. Apply your colors in a Stone pattern.

2. Begin your Gelgit by going back and forth one way.

3. Finish the Gelgit by repeating the back-and-forth motion in the opposite direction.

4. Make a Nonpareil.

5. Take your bouquet comb and move it in a gentle wave down the tray in the same direction as the comb used to create the Nonpareil.

6. Lay the paper, tap, and peel from the tray. Rinse gently and hang up to dry.

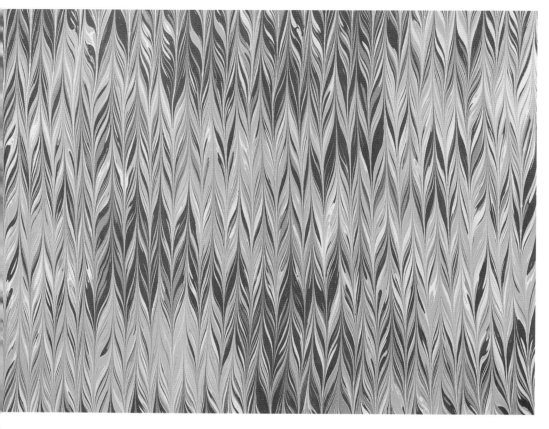

CHEVRON PATTERNS

A Chevron is very like a Gelgit, except much smaller and finer in detail. The last two passes require the use of a comb, which adds to the consistency of the lines. This example uses a 0.6 in. (1.5 cm) comb, though you can change the look of the pattern by experimenting with different widths. Since it takes some time to create, dust falling onto the pattern and making holes can become a problem. It is best to do this pattern quickly and, if you are able to, increase the humidity of your marbling space. You will also see fewer dust particles if you use acrylics rather than gouache or watercolor.

1. Apply your colors in a Stone pattern.

2. Make a Gelgit by using a stylus or a rake. Using a comb, make a Cascade pattern by drawing it across the tray in the opposite direction of the last pass of the Gelgit.

3. Using the same comb, move it along so the teeth are in between the last lines drawn. Push it back up the tray to the other end, bisecting the lines you have already drawn.

4. Lay the paper, tap, and peel from the tray. Rinse gently and hang up to dry.

PALM OR FERN

So called because of the way the lines drape like the fronds of the palm or fern, this pattern is beautifully fluid and intricate. This example is made using a 0.6 in. (1.5 cm) comb and a 1.2 in. (3 cm) rake. Try changing the width of the rake to get different effects. As with all Chevron-based patterns, the aim is to complete the pattern quickly and smoothly to avoid the issue of dust falling on the tray surface.

1. Apply your colors in a Stone pattern.

2. Make a Gelgit by using a stylus or a rake. Using a comb, make a Cascade pattern by drawing it across the tray in the opposite direction of the last pass of the Gelgit.

3. Using the same comb, move it along so the teeth are in between the last lines drawn. Push it back up the tray to the other end, bisecting the lines you have already drawn to create the Chevron.

4. Using a rake, draw across the tray at 90 degrees to the direction of the Chevron.

5. Lay the paper, tap, and lift from the tray. Rinse gently and hang up to dry.

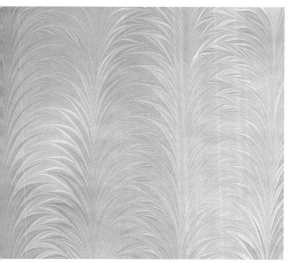

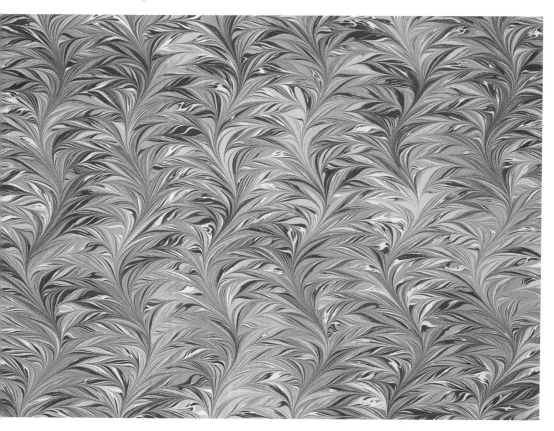

FLAME

Similar to the Palm or Fern, the Flame pattern has extra movement due to the wave in the last pass of the rake. This example is made using a 0.6 in. (1.5 cm) comb and a 1.2 in. (3 cm) rake, but you can change the width of the rake to get different effects. As with all Chevron-based patterns, the aim is to complete the pattern quickly and smoothly to avoid the issue of dust falling on the tray surface.

1. Apply your colors in a Stone pattern.

2. Make a Gelgit by using a stylus or a rake. Using a comb, make a Cascade pattern by drawing it across the tray in the opposite direction of the last pass of the Gelgit.

3. Using the same comb, move it along so the teeth are in between the last lines drawn. Push it back up the tray to the other end, bisecting the lines you have already drawn to create the Chevron.

4. Using a rake in a gentle wave motion, draw it across the tray at 90 degrees to the direction of the Chevron.

5. Lay the paper, tap, and lift from the tray. Rinse gently and hang up to dry.

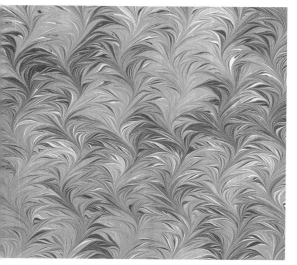

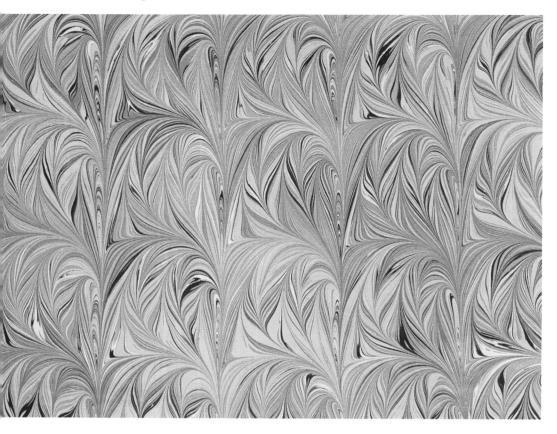

COCKATOO

An unusual but effective pattern evoking the plume of the cockatoo, this has its base in the Palm or Fern pattern. This example is made using a 0.6 in. (1.5 cm) comb and a 1.2 in. (3 cm) rake.

1. Apply your colors in a Stone pattern.

2. Make a Gelgit by using a stylus or a rake. Using a comb, make a Cascade pattern by drawing it across the tray in the opposite direction of the last pass of the Gelgit.

3. Using the same comb, move it along so the teeth are in between the last lines drawn. Push it back up the tray to the other end, bisecting the lines you have already drawn to create the Chevron.

4. Using a rake to create the Palm (or Fern), draw it across the tray at 90 degrees in the same direction as the Chevron.

5. Using the same rake, turn it 90 degrees and rake back across the whole tray.

6. Lay the paper, tap, and lift from the tray. Rinse gently and hang up to dry.

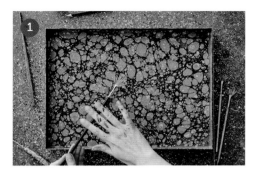

FLEUR-DE-LIS

This is another pattern that calls for the bouquet comb, and again the practice and effort to master this pattern is well worth it.

1. Apply your colors in a Stone pattern.

2. Make a Gelgit by using a stylus or a rake. Using a comb, make a Cascade pattern by drawing it across the tray in the opposite direction of the last pass of the Gelgit.

3. Using the same comb, move it along so the teeth are in between the last lines drawn. Push it back up the tray to the other end, bisecting the lines you have already drawn to create the Chevron.

4. Take your bouquet comb and move it in a gentle wave down the tray in the same direction as your Chevron.

5. Lay the paper, tap, and peel from the tray. Rinse gently and hang up to dry.

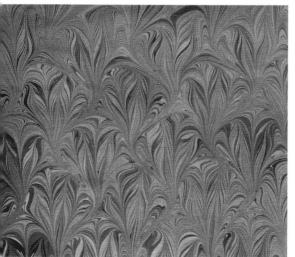

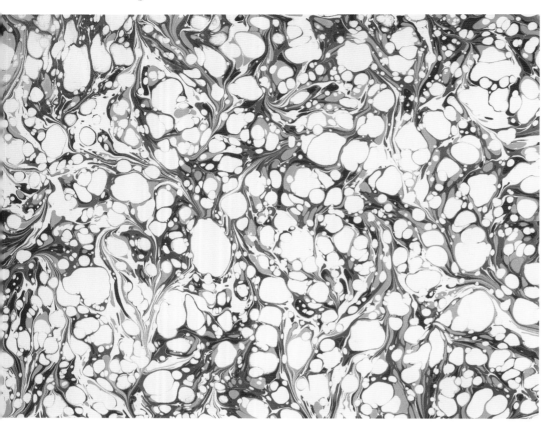

OTHER PATTERNS

ITALIAN VEIN

The Italian Vein is a versatile pattern that relies on negative space created by a very dilute dispersant sprinkled over it. You will need to water your dispersant down even further from the recipes given in this book, and play with different concentrations to get the right balance. You can use a solution of water and detergent, water and ox gall, or water and Photo Flo. You will also need to thin your paints so that when they are pushed into the tight veins, they don't get too concentrated and heavy and start to sink. Even worse, they might not adhere to your paper.

1. Create a Stone pattern.

2. With a stylus, randomly draw through your stone pattern. This step is optional.

3. Sprinkle the pattern with your solution of dispersant.

4. Lay your paper, tap, and peel off the bath. Rinse gently, concentrating on any areas where the paint may have become a little too concentrated. Hang up to dry.

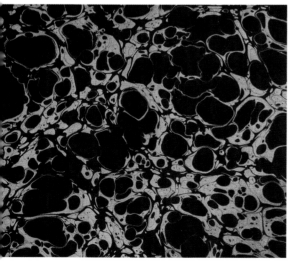

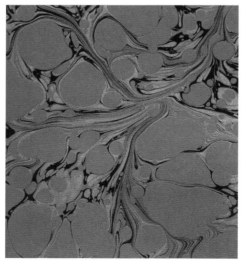

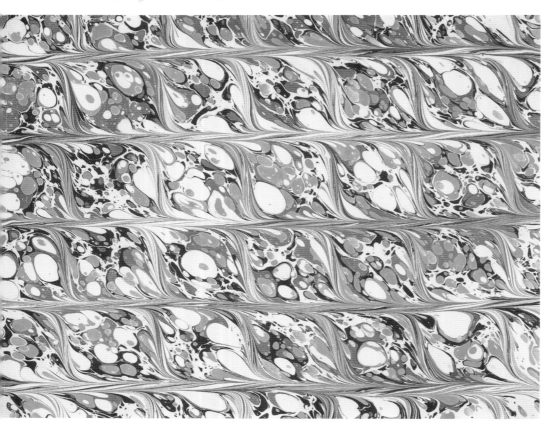

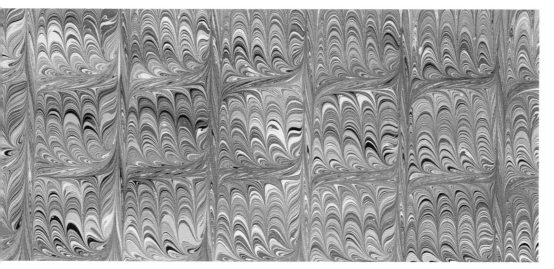

CABLE PATTERN

The Cable pattern is unusual since it is more of a pattern element than a pattern in itself, and it can be used on top of any other design. Where the rake lines pass so closely to one another, the thin threads of paint take on a twisted appearance. Shown here is the Double Cable over a Turkish Stone, using a 1.2 in. (3 cm) rake. Stopping at step 3 will give you a Single Cable. Try with a different pin spacing in your choice of rake to give the pattern a different appearance.

1. Apply your colors to the tray and complete whatever pattern you choose.

2. From the top of the tray, pull the rake through the pattern to the bottom.

3. At the bottom, shift your rake approximately 0.2 in. (5 mm) to one side. Push the rake back up the tray, taking care to follow evenly alongside your previous lines. End here for a Single Cable.

4. Using the same rake, turn it 90 degrees, then pull it from left to right across the pattern to make a Double Cable.

5. At the end of the tray, shift the rake approximately 0.2 in. (5 mm) to one side and push it back along the tray, keeping as evenly as before alongside your previous lines.

6. Lay the paper, tap, and peel from the tray. Rinse gently and hang up to dry.

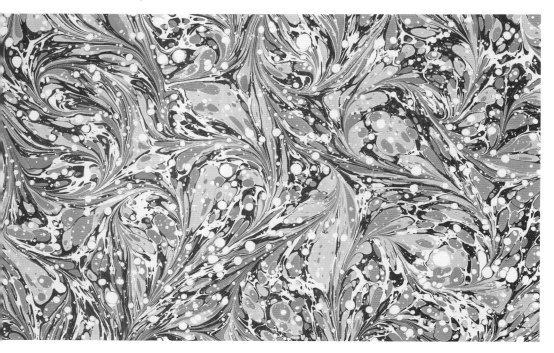

ANTIQUING

Another pattern element that can be applied to many designs is the technique of antiquing. A paper has been "antiqued" if very small stones are laid at the end over a pattern. Here are two examples.

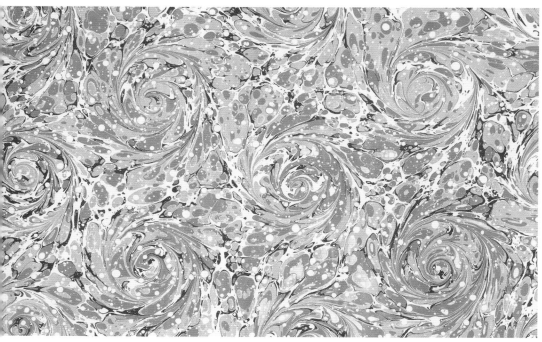

Antiqued Drawn Stone

1. Turkish Stone pattern

2. Use a stylus randomly to create a Drawn Stone pattern.

3. Throw tiny stones of a final color onto the pattern.

4. Lay the paper and pull the print from the tray.

Antiqued Snail

1. Turkish Stone pattern

2. Use a stylus to draw curls.

3. Throw tiny stones of a final color onto the pattern.

4. Lay the paper and pull the print from the tray.

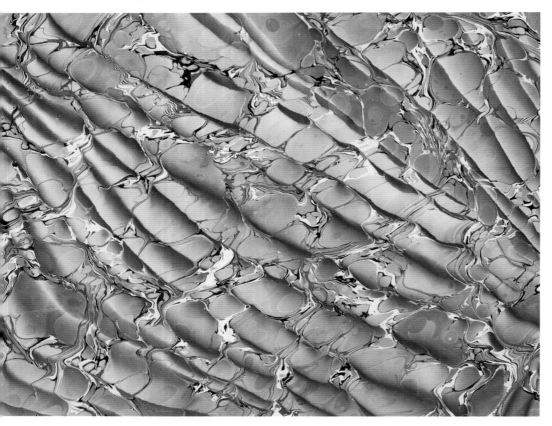

SPANISH WAVE

Perhaps the most illusory of patterns, the resulting papers often look like moving water or fabric. "Spanish Wave" refers to a technique that can be used on various patterns, and in its simplest form involves the shifting of the paper as it is laid onto the bath. The story goes that this technique was invented by a marbler who came to work still feeling the effects of the night before, and transferred the shaking of his hands to the paper as he marbled. Instead of being thrown out of a job, his ecstatic employer directed him to hone the technique. This example has been made over a Stone pattern, with the last color thrown on in large stones to increase the effect of the wave.

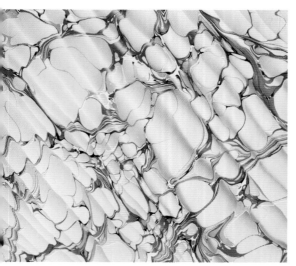

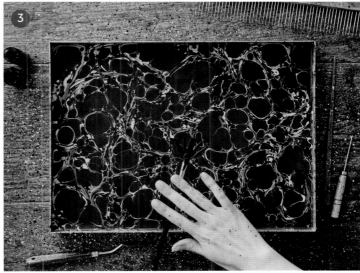

1. Apply your colors in a stone pattern.

2. Gently swirl the colors with a stylus. This step is optional.

3. Throw large stones of the last color over the bath.

4. Take a sheet of alummed paper and hold it in opposite corners. Put the first corner down a little farther than usual from the corner of the tray and begin a gentle back-and-forth motion. As you rock the paper, gradually lower it with your other hand. This will take practice to get the coordination right. Once the paper is down, tap and lift it from the tray.

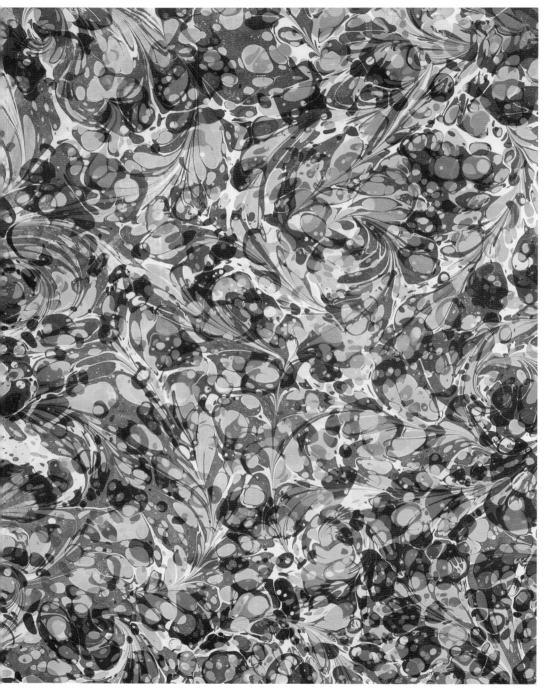

OVERMARBLE

This technique involves marbling again over a paper that has already been marbled. It is usually done twice, but more layers can be added. Depending on the translucency of the paints used, each layer can affect the next in fascinating ways. The first pattern must be dry and recoated with alum before the second pattern layer is added. The dried paper must be carefully treated with alum to ensure that none of the paint comes away—gentle sponging or misting with alum is best. It must then be allowed to dry and flatten in the same way as regular papers. Overmarbling is an excellent way of turning a paper you weren't thrilled by into something new and potentially beautiful.

1. Prepare a marbled sheet with alum and have it dry and ready to use. In your marbling tray, create a new pattern. This example shows a Drawn Stone.

2. Retrieve your premarbled and alummed sheet. Here I chose a simple Stone pattern that was a little pale and faded in places.

3. Lay your marbled sheet onto the bath.

4. Peel the print off the bath, rinse gently, and hang up to dry.

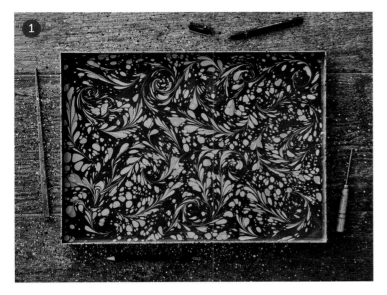

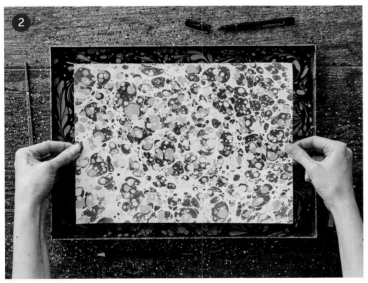

OVERMARBLING USING NEGATIVE SPACE

Overmarbling doesn't have to be complex or busy to be effective. This example shows the use of a single gold color to help lift a print that was a little dull and lackluster.

1. Apply a thin layer of gold to the *size* all around the tray.

2. Sprinkle the gold with dispersant to make an Italian Vein.

3. The premarbled sheet—in this case a Drawn Stone with unbalanced colors

4. Lay the paper and pull the print from the tray.

The result is a rather lovely paper.

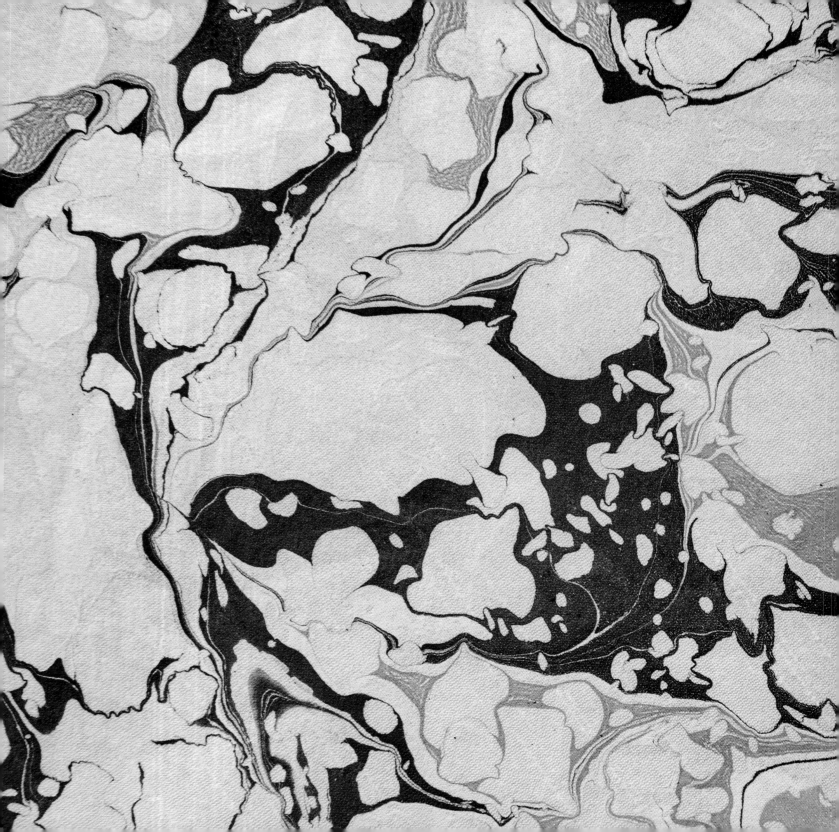

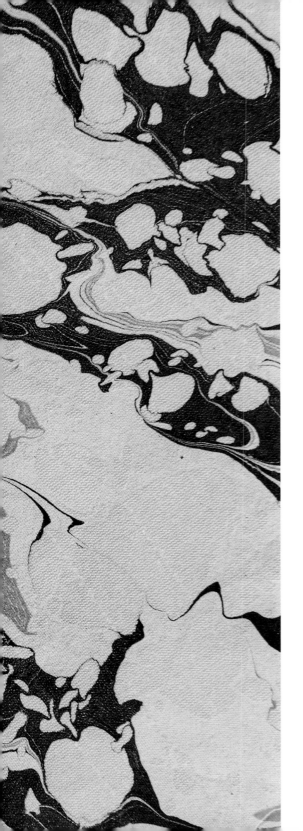

FABRIC
MARBLING

PREPARATION AND TECHNIQUES

There is something rather special and luxurious about this technique of transferring the currents and swirls of paint onto cloth. Perhaps it is the harmonious way in which the material also flows and gathers that just seems to make fabric and marbling the perfect pairing.

Happily, the differences between marbling on paper and marbling on fabric are few. You will need to spend a little more time in preparation and, perhaps, in finding the best materials to work on, but once you start it is difficult not to fall in love with this way of printing.

TOOLS

- Blender or mixer for making *size* (if using carrageenan)
- Bucket or large container
- Gloves
- Paint applicators: whisks, brushes, pipettes, eyedroppers
- Pots or jars for mixing paint
- Rakes and combs—optional
- Styluses
- Tray to fit the size of your fabric

MATERIALS

- Acrylic paint
- Alum
- Fabric
- *Size*—carrageenan or methocel

This list of tools and materials is very similar to what you need for paper marbling. The only two bits of equipment that you will need to think about are the tray and the container in which you will prepare your fabric. You will need to carefully consider both in the light of the size and quantity of fabric you are hoping to marble.

The type and size of tray will depend completely on the size of fabric you want to marble. You may want to marble scarves, in which case your tray will need to be long and thin. If you don't want to immediately invest in a large bespoke tray, or you plan on marbling only a few large pieces occasionally, you can always make a temporary one. The best way to do this is to buy a few long lengths of inexpensive wood and cut them into batons. Glue or nail them together into a frame. Next, lower a thick plastic sheet over the frame. You can always tape this to the frame or to the table or bench you are working on. Fill the plastic-lined frame with *size* and you are good to go.

CHOOSING *SIZE*

Both carrageenan and methocel make good *sizes* for marbling fabric—because the paints used are acrylics, you have the choice. Some prefer carrageenan because they like the control they have over their paints. On the other hand, methocel can be easier to wash out of the fabric and is less expensive if you plan on marbling large pieces. It also is less likely to be spoiled quickly by the acrylic paints. In the examples that follow, a carrageenan *size* has been used.

CHOOSING FABRIC

As with paper, often the choice will come down to budget and intended use. It may surprise you to know that you can marble on lots of different types of fabric. Silk has long been the favorite material of many marblers because of the vibrancy of color and the crispness of pattern that it allows.

Natural fibers, such as cotton, have also been favored, although linen rather less so, since the patterns tend to lose clarity on the looser weave of the material. It is also possible to marble onto cotton blends, silk blends, rayon, polyesters, and even newer materials such as modern cork fabrics. I have had success with all of these materials, but the key, as with paper, is to test whatever material you are hoping to use first.

PREPARING FABRIC

Before marbling onto whatever fabric you have chosen, it is important to wash it to remove anything that might prevent your mordant from being applied evenly. If it is cut from the bolt, wash around 3 feet at a time with a little gentle detergent. Dry the fabric well, either on a line (imperative for silk) or in a dryer. Once it's dry, you can iron the fabric if needed.

You will need to mordant the fabric with alum to ensure that your paint will stick. Make sure to do this in a well-ventilated area and wear gloves to protect your skin. For materials like cork fabric, you can alum with a sponge in the same way as you would marble a sheet of paper, then either hang to dry or dry flat. For all other types, you will need to put your fabric into a bucket or container large enough for the amount you wish to marble, then soak it in alum. For most fabrics I have marbled on, I have found the solution described earlier in the book for paper marbling to be adequate, with the very rare exception. You will, however, need to increase the amount of alum from the recipe so that there is enough to adequately soak the amount of fabric you intend to marble. You can either work this out or make up a few small batches until your fabric is well covered in the container. You will need to leave it to soak for at least twenty minutes to allow it to become completely saturated. After this, you can remove it from the bucket or container and hang it up to dry. If possible, it's best not to wring it out, but to leave it to drip-dry so that you're not adding lots of extra creases.

Once it's dry, you can flatten the fabric with an iron (no steam), if needed, to remove any large creases. Fine wrinkles will often not cause any issues. Your fabric is now ready to marble on.

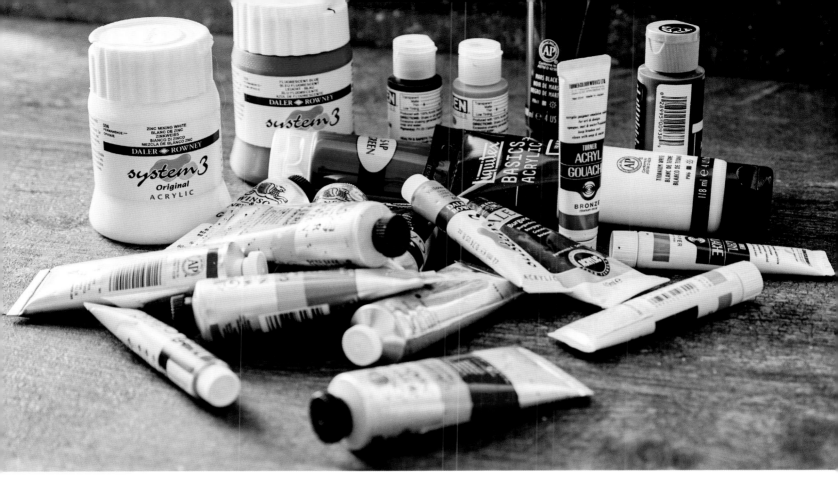

PAINT

The best paint for fabric marbling is undoubtedly acrylic, since it produces resilient, varied, vibrant patterns. They can be mixed up in exactly the same way as for paper marbling.

Most acrylics will set on a dry fabric with heat and can then be handwashed with gentle soap—but do test your chosen paint brand first. For added longevity, or if your paints do not stick after being washed, you can mix your paints with an acrylic medium designed for use on fabric. Fabric mediums are made by many different brands, including Liquitex and Daler Rowney. These will come with instructions for the amount to mix with

your paint (often 1:1). You may find this is enough to thin your paint to marbling consistency. If not, thin it down a little with distilled or soft water.

You can marble onto fabric with other paints, including oil, fabric paints, gouache, and watercolor. The trick—as with any type of marbling paint—is to get them balanced enough to float and spread. You will find with gouache and watercolor that they are far more likely to wash off during rinsing if you are not careful. Fabrics marbled using gouache and watercolor cannot be washed once dry, since you will wash away your paint.

LAYING FABRIC

Depending on the size of your fabric, the way to lay it on the tray will be different. For small pieces, you can just hold the fabric at opposite corners and lower it onto the bath. You can see this in the following examples. For larger pieces you may need two people, especially for laying long pieces such as scarves. Each person will need to take an end and gently lower the fabric onto the *size* from the middle outward. If there is no one to help, you can either back the fabric with paper by pinning it, use a low-tack mounting spray, or attach a length of dowel along two opposite edges. The easiest way of doing this is to wrap a small amount of the fabric over and around the dowel and attach it to itself with pins. You can then hold the ends of both dowels and lay the fabric down easily from the middle outward.

AFTER MARBLING

Once your fabric is marbled, you will need to remove it carefully from the tray by using either a stick or a board. You can pull your fabric up and over the edge of the tray and slide it out. This can help remove some of the *size* from the surface of the fabric, but it can also cause marks in the pattern. It is best to experiment to see what works best for you. You must then rinse the fabric very carefully in a bucket of water to wash away any *size* that is clinging to it. Resist the urge to rub the marbled surface to get rid of the *size*, or you might end up washing away some of the paint. Instead, just swirl it gently. If the *size* is not rinsing off, you can try using some warm water. When it's rinsed, hang your fabric to dry. Once it's dried, you should iron it and set the paints. After a few days, it will be completely fine to handwash with gentle soap when needed.

Fabric Marbling

This section is designed to show you ways of making patterns on fabric by using acrylic paints. The fabrics used here are silk, polyester silk, cotton satin, and linen. Each fabric marbles differently, and I have tried to explain why I have chosen a certain pattern and the method used to make it.

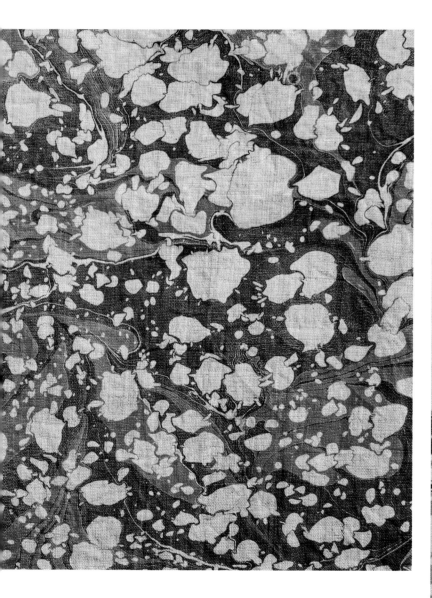

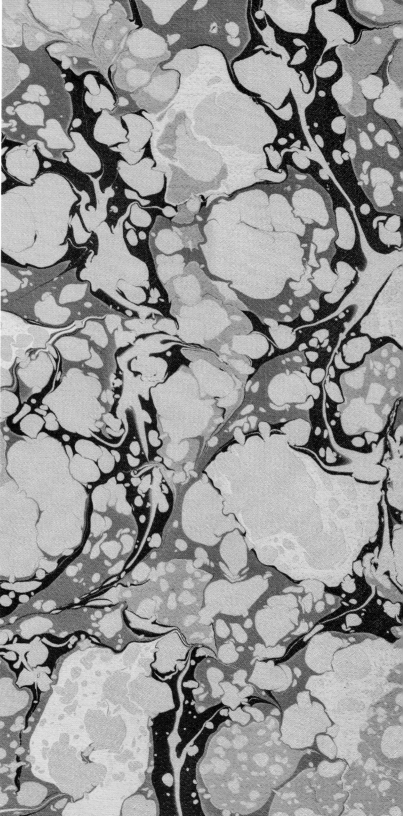

MARBLING ON SILK

For many people silk is the best fabric for marbling. The silk I am using is pure silk, and it can be bought for marbling purposes from specialist art stores ready-made into handkerchiefs, scarves, bandannas, etc., or in lengths from the bolt at good fabric stores and online retailers. It is an especially good choice if you want really bright, vibrant colors. It is also a good fabric to use if you want to make fine, detailed patterns, since the weave is very tight and the individual threads do not fluff and blur the patterns.

BULL'S-EYE ON SILK

This example shows a fine marbled pattern made with the bull's-eye method of applying paint with an eyedropper or pipette. The silk used here is a premade silk handkerchief with hand-rolled hems.

1. Begin by dropping one color at regular intervals in lines on the bath. Follow this by dropping more colors, one by one, into the centers of the first stones. Wait for each paint to stop spreading before applying the next color.

2. Continue building the regimented Stone pattern with more colors. Colors can be used more than once to increase their presence in the pattern—notably the yellow here.

3. The start of a Gelgit, using a stylus. Notice how much more consistent the colors appear over the pattern as opposed to throwing paint from a brush.

4. The completed Gelgit

5. Make a Cascade with a 0.4 in. (1 cm) comb.

6. Hold the fabric by its corners above the tray and gently lower it from the middle outward onto the *size*.

7. The silk handkerchief on the *size*

8. The finished print ready to rinse

FLAME PATTERN ON SILK

These pictures explain the random dropper method of applying paint. The pattern is an intricate Flame pattern (see page 120). The fabric is a lightweight Habotai silk, which takes the color and the print beautifully.

1. Begin by dropping one color randomly all over the bath until the surface is flooded. Continue in the same random manner inside the drops for the next color.

2. Continue building the random Stone pattern with more colors.

3. Use a stylus to create a Gelgit pattern.

4. Make a Cascade pattern by using a 0.4 in. (1 cm) comb.

5. Bisect the Cascade lines with the same comb to create a Chevron.

6. With a 1.2 in. (3 cm) rake used in a wave motion, create the Flame pattern.

7. Hold the silk by the corners and lay it down from the middle outward.

8. The finished print ready to rinse

FANTASY PATTERN ON SILK

Silk can also be used to create larger patterns too. The advantage of dropping paint with a pipette or eye dropper is that often the stones are bigger, which allows much more specific manipulation of the circles, as shown in this bright Fantasy pattern.

1. Begin by dropping one color randomly all over the bath until the surface is flooded. Continue dropping color in the same random manner for the next color.

2. Continue building the random Stone pattern with more colors.

3. Carefully drop the last color in large stones at random intervals—ideally so that they don't touch or melt into each other.

4. Use a stylus to create a pattern by concentrating on the last large stones. Even the beginning of a loose Gelgit here is turning the last blue stones into very specific, almost birdlike shapes.

5. Continue using the stylus in a random but controlled way to draw through and tease the large stone blobs into flowery, leaflike shapes.

6. Hold the silk by the corners and lay it down from the middle outward.

7. The finished print ready to rinse

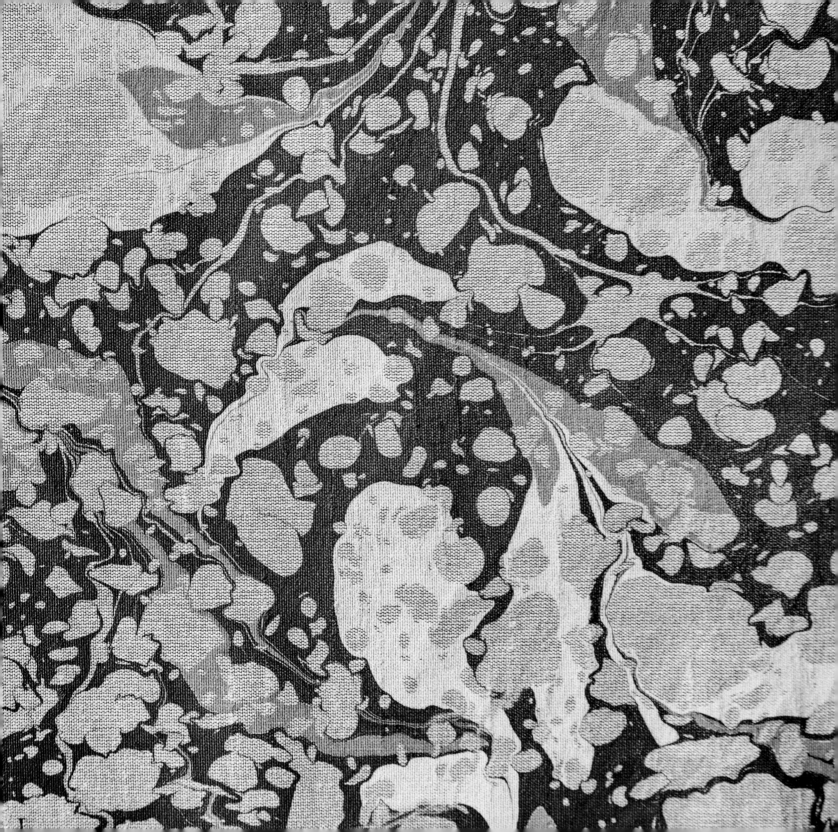

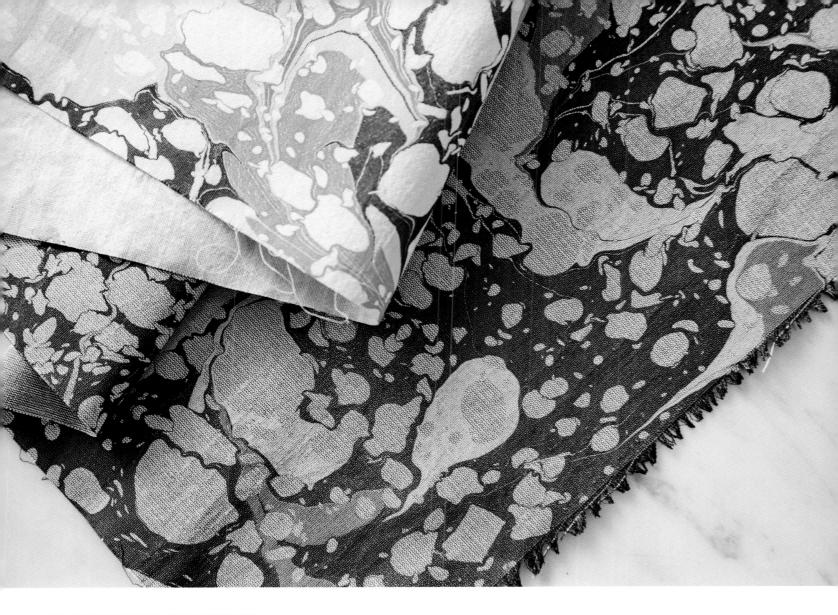

MARBLING ON POLYESTER

The fabric used in these examples is a mildly shiny polyester silk with a slight slub (uneven thickness). The fabric has a texture and is already quite decorative in itself. These three examples show the ways in which I have tried to choose the best patterns to complement the material.

RANDOM STONE ON POLYESTER

This used the Random Stone technique and a fairly intricate Feather pattern in the direction of the slub. The thought behind this was that the slub would add to the feathery effect, since any paint that did not adhere properly would become paler and fluffier over time—perhaps emulating the downy ends of a feather. Time will tell whether this is successful or not!

1. Begin by dropping colors randomly over the bath.

2. Continue building with more colors, but waiting each time for the previous color to stop expanding before adding the next.

3. Start a Gelgit by using a stylus.

4. The completed Gelgit

5. Make a Nonpareil by using a 0.2 in. (0.5 cm) comb.

6. Draw against the lines of the Nonpareil with a 1.2 in. (3 cm) rake.

7. With the same rake, push back up the tray, bisecting the last lines drawn.

8. Lay the fabric on the *size*.

9. The finished print ready to rinse

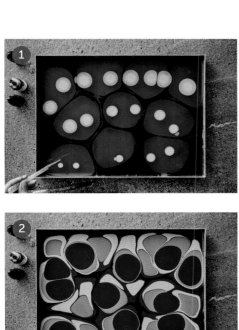

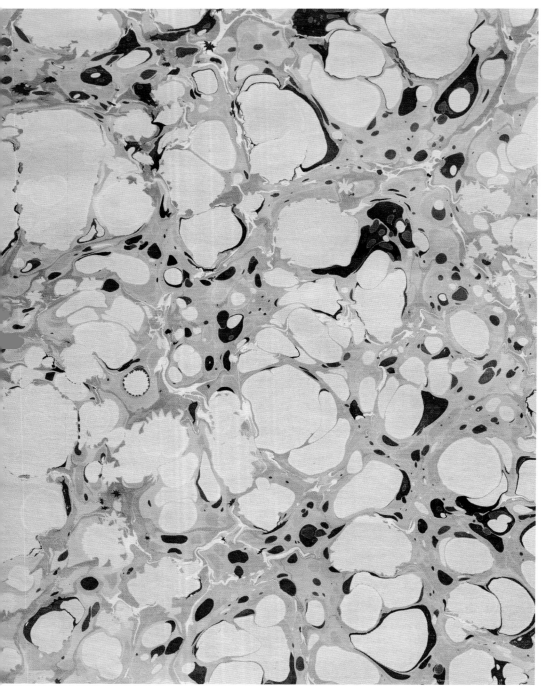

STONE PATTERN ON POLYESTER

Applying paint with a whisk can be an excellent way of producing Stone patterns. This example shows the use of a brush as well. I chose a muted palette to complement the pale ivory fabric, and used paints that are fairly translucent, in order to be able to retain the visual element of the slub underneath. The final print shows that some stones have started to take on a ragged, starlike appearance. This is often undesirable, especially in fine-combed patterns, and is a sign that the *size* or the paints are old or contaminated (or the paints just don't like the order in which they were laid). In this instance, however, I don't feel they detract from the pattern, and the odd shapes add to the organic, random, stonelike effect.

1. Use a whisk and tap it on a stick or rod to sprinkle paint randomly onto the bath. The strength with which you tap and the height from which the paint falls will have an effect on how the colors land and spread.

2. Continue building with more colors, waiting for the previous color to stop expanding before adding the next. These colors have been chosen for their transparency when transferred onto a material.

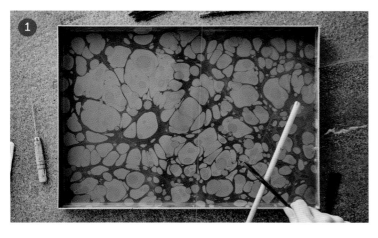

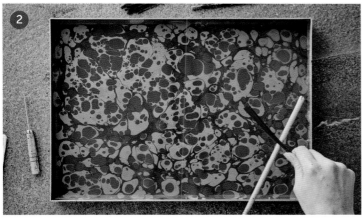

3. Use a brush to deliver larger stones of a very diluted color. This allows larger areas of the textured fabric to be seen through the pattern.

4. Lay the fabric on the *size* from the middle outward.

5. The finished print ready to rinse

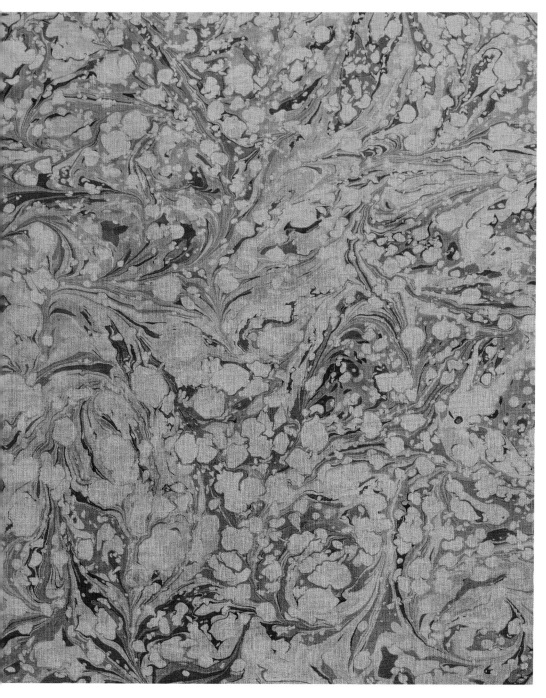

MASKING

Sometimes it is desirable to keep some areas of fabric free from paint and pattern in order to see the texture or color. There is no better way of doing this than using a masking technique, in this case a dilute dispersant, to create negative space within a pattern. This example uses an Italian Vein pattern (see page 126) to retain a little of the shine and the slub of the fabric. The paints have been diluted, and not much has been applied to the bath, so that the color of the fabric has a desaturating effect on the paint hues.

1. Use a whisk and tap it on a stick or rod to sprinkle paint randomly onto the bath. The strength with which you tap and the height from which the paint falls will have an effect on how the colors land and spread. Sprinkle sparingly to help keep the paints translucent.

2. Draw randomly through the pattern to break up the stones.

3. Use a brush to sprinkle some very dilute dispersant over the pattern. Adjust the concentration of the dispersant to vary the size of the spaces created.

4. Lay the fabric on the *size* from the middle outward.

5. The finished print ready to rinse

MARBLING ON SATIN

Satin is a fabric that typically has a very shiny front and a dull back. In fact, satin is actually the name of the weave rather than a type of fabric, and as such, many fibers can be used to make it; for example, silks and cottons. I chose this example of fabric to show that even very highly shiny materials can marble well.

Satin is a great candidate for using masking or negative-space techniques. However, for this example, I've used a hand-drawn pattern so that the fabric shows through in soft lines around the curls and at intervals across the fabric, much as if a metallic paint had been used for the job.

1. Begin by dropping one color at regular intervals in lines on the bath. Follow this by dropping more colors one by one into the centers of the first stones. Be patient and wait for each paint to stop spreading before applying the next.

2. Continue building the regimented Stone pattern with more colors. Colors can be used more than once to increase their presence in the pattern. This is often most effective with bright colors.

3. Start a Gelgit by using a stylus. Notice how much more consistent the colors appear over the area of the pattern, as opposed to throwing paint from a brush.

4. The nearly complete Gelgit

5. Draw curls in the pattern between the lines of the Gelgit at regular intervals.

6. Hold the fabric by its corners above the tray and gently lower it from the middle outward onto the *size*.

7. The finished print ready to rinse

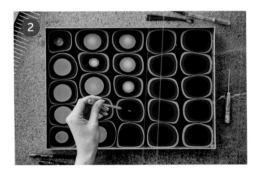

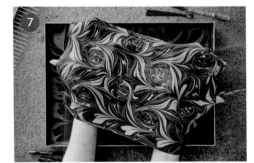

MARBLING ON LINEN

Linen is a natural fabric made from flax, although you often find it blended with cotton and silk. It is generally considered a poor fabric to marble on because of its more open weave and textured surface. However, it is for these very reasons that I like it.

Some linens can have quite a close weave and a very fine texture, albeit not at all like a fine silk or cotton. These linens marble well if properly washed and treated first and used with patterns that are not too detailed or combed.

More heavily textured linens can also be marbled, although you may find that the paint does not always adhere as well. You can use this to your advantage and create pieces that have a patchy, aged look to them.

I used a midtextured linen in this example and a regular but hand-drawn pattern. The finished piece should age well over time, giving a gentle, worn appearance.

1. Begin by dropping one color at regular intervals in lines on the bath. Follow this by dropping more colors one by one into the centers of the first stones. Wait for each paint color to stop spreading before going on to apply the next.

2. Continue building the regimented Stone pattern with more colors. Remember that if you like, colors can be used more than once to increase their presence in the pattern.

3. Start working up a Gelgit with a stylus.

4. Draw through large patches of color to create uneven, floral shapes.

5. Hold the fabric by its corners above the tray and gently lower it from the middle outward onto the *size*.

6. The fabric on the bath, showing the heavily textured surface. The thickness of the material stops the pattern from showing through.

7. The finished print ready to rinse

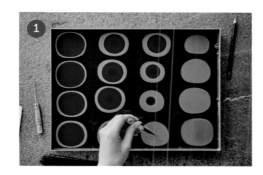

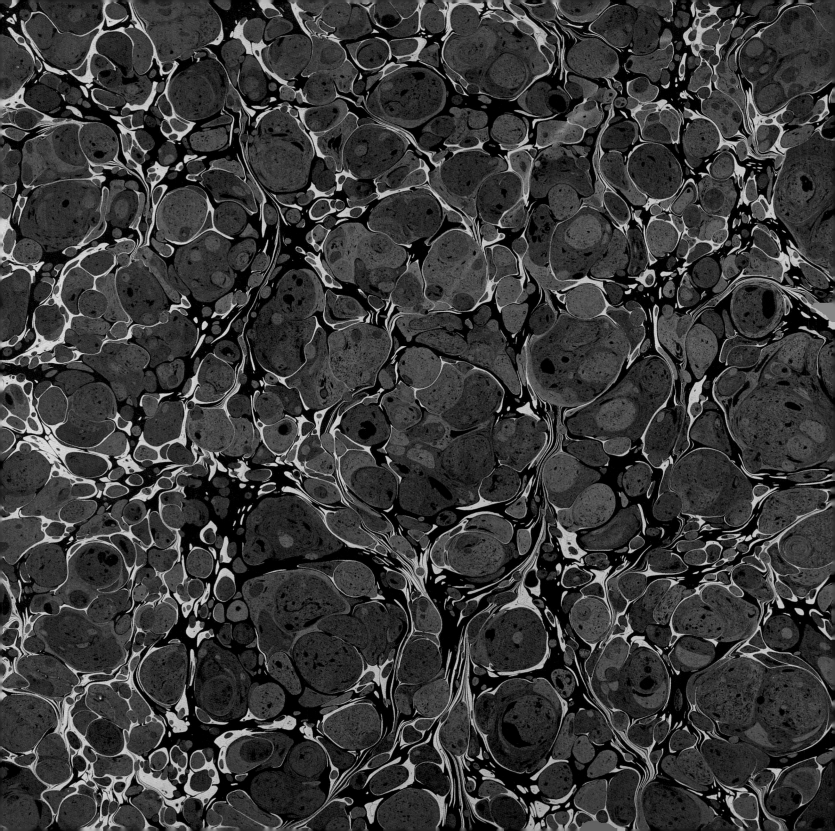

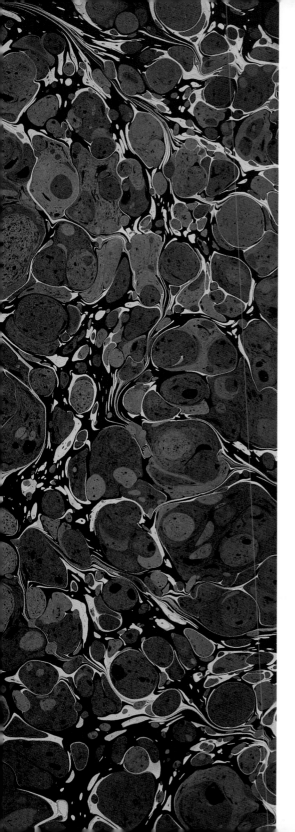

TROUBLESHOOTING

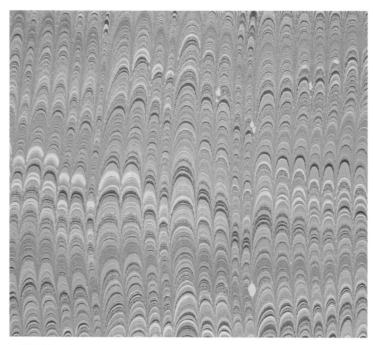

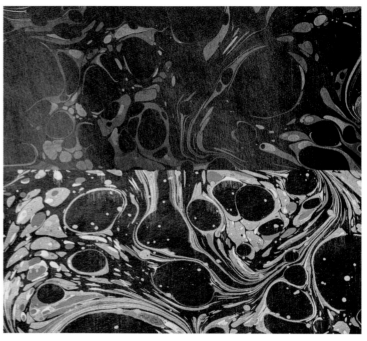

SMALL SPECKS AND HOLES APPEAR IN THE PATTERN

- Made by dust or small fibers from clothes falling onto the *size*. Print quickly and avoid the amount of time your hands and arms move over the tray.

- Minute air bubbles in the *size* can also cause holes. Skim well before throwing paint into the tray. Stir your paint carefully, without making bubbles that could transfer onto your bath.

- Dust or small alum crystals on the paper. Be sure to alum evenly and don't overwet the paper with it. Keep the paper between boards until just before you need it, to avoid any airborne matter settling on it.

- Paint granules. If your paint sits for too long without being agitated, the pigment particles can fall out of suspension or clump together. Stir your paint well every time you use it.

PAINT RUNNING OFF PAPER

- The paper may not have been coated with alum correctly, or the wrong side of the paper was used to make a print. Be sure to alum evenly, and check which side of the paper you are laying onto the bath!

- Too much paint was laid on the bath. The mordanted paper can hold only so much—try not to overload the *size* with paint. Remember, even if it appears pale in the tray, the colors often look much brighter on the paper.

- The paints were too thick. The buildup of pigment can be too much for the paper to hold. Make sure your colors are diluted and spreading well.

- Rarely, the problem might be the paper itself. It may have a coating or internal sizing that means it cannot absorb alum and therefore cannot hold the paint.

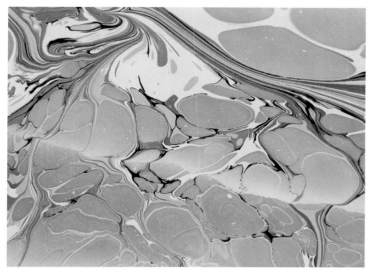

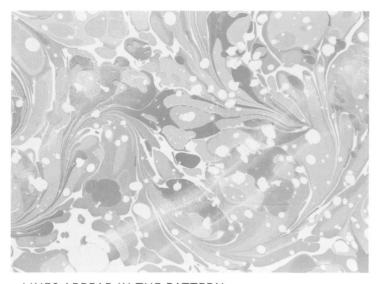

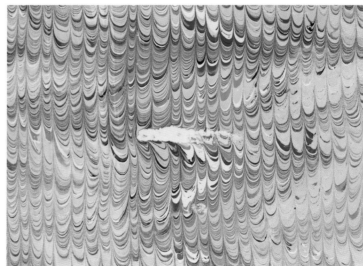

LINES APPEAR IN THE PATTERN

- These are "hesitation" lines, often caused by unintentional movement of the paper when it was laid on the bath. Be sure to lay your paper smoothly. Holding the first corner laid on the *size* throughout can also stop unwanted movement.

BLOTCHY AREAS / PAINT NOT ADHERING

- The most likely reason is that the alum was still wet when the paper was laid down. Make sure all your papers are dry and flat before using.

- Sometimes the type of paper can cause these problems. A coating or internal sizing can inhibit the absorption of the alum.

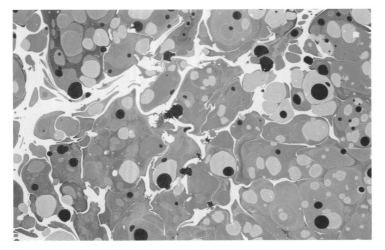

- Paint is contaminated. Make sure all brushes and paint containers are clean before mixing paints. Sometimes it is the chemicals in one paint reacting with another. If it happens only with particular combinations, either change color schemes or swap in another brand of paint.

PAINT FORMS JAGGED OR FUZZY EDGES

- The *size* has become contaminated by chemicals in the paints or by alum. Skim well to clean the surface before beginning to marble. If the problem continues, stir the *size* carefully and skim again. If you can, add a little water as well, as long as it doesn't ruin the consistency. If the problem continues, throw it out and make fresh *size*.

- The *size* is old. Replace with fresh.

- The *size* is immature. Sometimes the bath needs to warm up a bit before paints will behave smoothly. Often the second day of marbling will produce better results, since the *size* has been seasoned by the previous day's paints.

- The *size* is too cold. Wait for it to come to room temperature (especially if it has been in the fridge) or add a little warm water (as long as the consistency is not ruined).

- A skin has formed on the *size*. This can be due to the fact that the surface has not been skimmed in a while, or if the air is too dry. Try to avoid having your tray in a draft, and increase humidity where possible.

LARGE HOLES APPEAR IN PATTERN

- The most likely cause is that an air bubble was trapped under the paper when it was laid, so that part of the paper didn't touch the paint. Be sure that your paper is flat before rolling it smoothly onto the *size*, one corner to the diagonal corner. Try not to drop your paper, but lay it down purposefully.

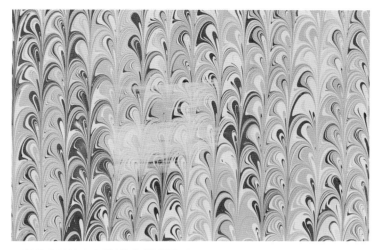

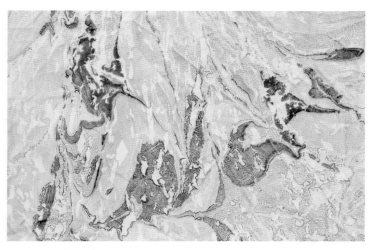

STREAKS IN THE PATTERN

- Most likely caused by an uneven coating of alum. Be sure to coat papers evenly and not to use your sponge too dry.

PAINT CRACKING

- Not always a problem, this can be used deliberately to create interesting patterns. It is most likely caused by paint drying on the surface of the *size*, although some paints naturally have clumping pigments. To use this as a deliberate effect, create a pattern and then leave it for some time to dry and break down.

- To avoid it, however, you will need to either increase the humidity of your space or reduce the amount of time the paint has to dry on the surface of the *size*, by working quickly.

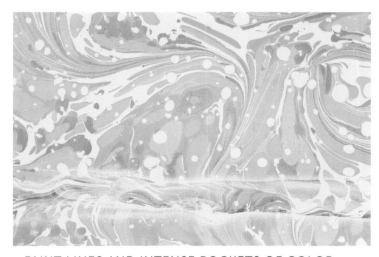

FAINT LINES AND INTENSE POCKETS OF COLOR

- This occurs when an air bubble has been trapped under the paper when it was laid, but has then been dislodged by tapping the back of the paper. Avoid trapping air bubbles!

ARTISTS

I have included this section to introduce you to a few marbling artists working professionally today (and it is certainly not an exhaustive list!). The thing I find fascinating is how each artist is able to discover their own style of marbling due to the variable nature of the craft and the different types of materials that can be used. Despite there being some regularity about producing certain patterns, each marbling artist will produce it in their own way, and therefore two patterns that are technically the same can look wildly different. And of course, there are still new patterns and discoveries being made, and appreciating the work of other practitioners can ultimately lead you to push the boundaries of your own practice. Here are a few places to start!

GRIFFIN BENKO

Griffin Benko is a marbling artist from Chicago, Illinois. He primarily marbles using acrylic paints and produces papers that he also turns into other goods such as coasters, books, and jewelry. Marbling flat-brim hats has become a recent fascination for him. He says of marbling: "There's something so enjoyable about producing truly unique marbled goods that people can wear or use in daily life. My favorite thing about marbling is how much it has opened up the artistic and creative side of my life. It also helps to put me into a 'flow state' where I find myself losing track of time. I'll find that five hours have passed and I'll be surrounded by tons of brand-new marbled goods (and probably be ready for a snack). This art form gives me great feelings of accomplishment as well as the desire to continue exploring and learning more beyond just the world of marbling."

Griffin Benko marbles onto an array of materials and products.

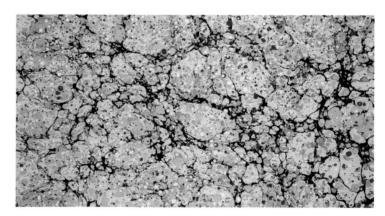

Turkish Stone pattern using acrylic paints.

Palm pattern made using acrylic paints.

CHENA RIVER MARBLERS

Regina and Daniel St. John are a married marbling team, working together as Chena River Marblers. The name Chena River is derived from a river located in the interior region of Alaska, where for sixteen years the St. Johns worked as educators in three teacher schools in remote villages as well as in Fairbanks. Marbling entered their life after their return to New England in 1985. In time, Regina found that her true inclination was to marble bold, contemporary, multilayered patterns, using acrylic paints. Dan was drawn to the traditional watercolor marbling as it was done 250 years ago, with a paint embedded with a beeswax paste and chemical additives. His extensive background in chemistry, physics, and woodworking has added significantly to understanding the process and having top-quality equipment to work with. Dan's inventive combs allowed for an explosion of extraordinary new patterns, and his mastery of the classical watercolor marbling allows them to explore and to teach a whole range of exciting marbling techniques.

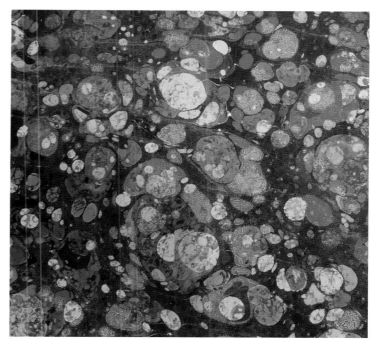

Purposeful overmarble.

A pattern created by a comb named the Italian Sisters.

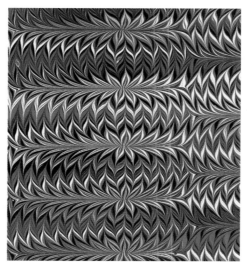

Chrysanthemum pattern invented by Galen Berry.

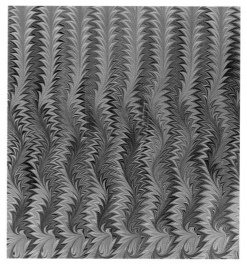

Teaching sampler, showing patterns palm, flame and octopus.

KATE BRETT

Kate started experimenting with making marbled papers in a drafty barn in Payhembury, Devon, in 1982 after attending a two-year bookbinding course. Inspired by old papers in antique books, Kate began a process of trial and error until she was able to reproduce some of the more traditional designs such as Old Dutch, Antique Spot, and French Curl. Kate's life has proven that one of the joys of marbling is that it is easily transportable. After starting her business in Payhembury, she then moved to Scotland and used to collect the carragheen for making the *size* from the western coasts surrounding the islands. She then married a man she met there, who is involved in rhino conservation. Years in Kenya, Zimbabwe, and Botswana followed. Her customers have become accustomed to receiving parcels from far-flung places! These days they often spend most of the summer in the Outer Hebrides. Kate says of marbling, "After all this time I still find marbling a very calming and meditative occupation. If all the elements involved in its manufacture are working together well, the drawing of the sheet from the tray can be a pleasant surprise."

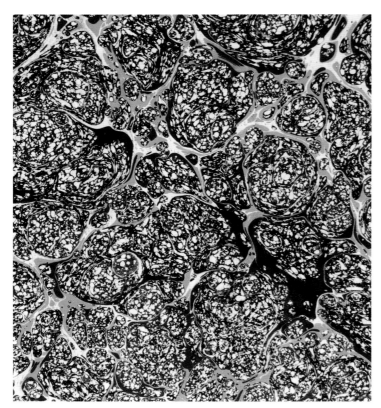

Kate Brett is a skilled reproducer of historical marbled patterns, such as this Stormont pattern.

An example of a pattern known as Old Dutch.

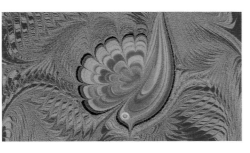

Bird of Ray.

James Mouland uses traditional ebru techniques to paint pictures on water.

Red Gloster pattern.

Contemporary marbled paper using gouache paints.

RACHEL MAIDEN

Rachel is a paper-marbling artist and owner of Maiden Marbling, a studio based in Cheshire, UK. Her interest in marbled papers grew out of her love of books and an interest in textile and surface design, which began during her education at art college. After spending some time assisting in a bindery, she spent two years mastering the craft, learning from practicing marblers and hours spent marbling hundreds of sheets of paper on her kitchen table. She was determined to master many of the historical patterns by using the traditional method of "throwing" down color onto carrageenan size. Later she developed her style, and along with the traditional, her interest lies in contemporary designs and rich colors. A favored area of work is creating bespoke patterns and experimenting with color matching in her design work. Her designs have been licensed for publishers, graphic designers, and interior designers, as well as artists and craft makers. Rachel is also keen to keep the craft alive and teaches at Westhope Crafts College in partnership with the Heritage Crafts Association.

JAMES MOULAND

James is an English artist married to a Turkish wife, raising two lively young children. He learned his craft in Istanbul, studying for five years with *ebru* master Kubilay Dinçer, and now teaches, designs, and sells from Hotwalls Studios, Portsmouth City's creative hub. His products are based on his original work and include pure silk scarves, poncho-style tops, cards, and cushions. When teaching, he enjoys seeing people experience the magic of marbling for the first time: "I take students through the process step by step, ensuring absolute beginners produce work they are proud of." He says of marbling, "It is such a wonderful process—frustrating at times, but ultimately very rewarding. I love the anticipation of imagining a new design and then planning the process to make it happen."

GLOSSARY

alum: An abbreviation of aluminum potassium sulphate. It is used as a mordant to coat paper and fabric and help the marbled patterns stick.

carrageenan: An extract of seaweed (Irish moss) that is used to thicken water to make a marbling *size*

comb: A marbling tool usually made of a length of wood with pins at regular intervals. Teeth are spaced more narrowly than those in a rake.

dispersant: A chemical substance added to a diluted paint to help it break the surface tension of the *size* when it is applied

methocel: A mixture of water and methylcellulose (a wood pulp extract) used to thicken water to make a marbling *size*

rake: A marbling tool usually made of a length of wood with pins at regular intervals. Teeth are spaced wider apart than those in a comb.

size: Thickened water substance used to fill the marbling tray, onto which paints or inks are dropped to make patterns (in *italics* throughout)

whisk: Paint applicator made by bunching strands of broomcorn or bristle

SUPPLIERS

PAPER AND PAINT

Shepherds Bookbinders (*www.bookbinding.co.uk*)
A leading retailer of fine papers, they have an online store and a physical store in Victoria, London. The store is a paper addict's paradise, and their shop assistants are extremely knowledgeable.

Cass Art (*www.cassart.co.uk*)
High-quality and affordable art supplies, such as paints and papers suitable for marbling. They have physical stores in London, Bristol, Liverpool, Manchester, Edinburgh, Glasgow, Brighton, Birmingham, Winchester, and Leeds.

Jackson's Art Supplies (*www.jacksonart.com*)
Papers suitable for marbling as well as high-quality, affordable paints, including their own range of watercolors and acrylics

S. R. Stevenson (*www.stuartstevenson.co.uk*)
A gorgeous little store in London, their range of paints and papers is impressive, and the staff is very knowledgeable. They have an online store and also take orders by telephone.

The SAA (*www.saa.co.uk*)
The Society for All Artists. An impressive array of paints and papers online. You can become a member for further discounts.

OTHER MARBLING SUPPLIES

Jacquard Products (*www.jacquardproducts.com*)
Supplier of marbling colors, carrageenan, methocel, synthetic ox gall, and alum. They also produce a marbling kit. They have distributors worldwide and online.

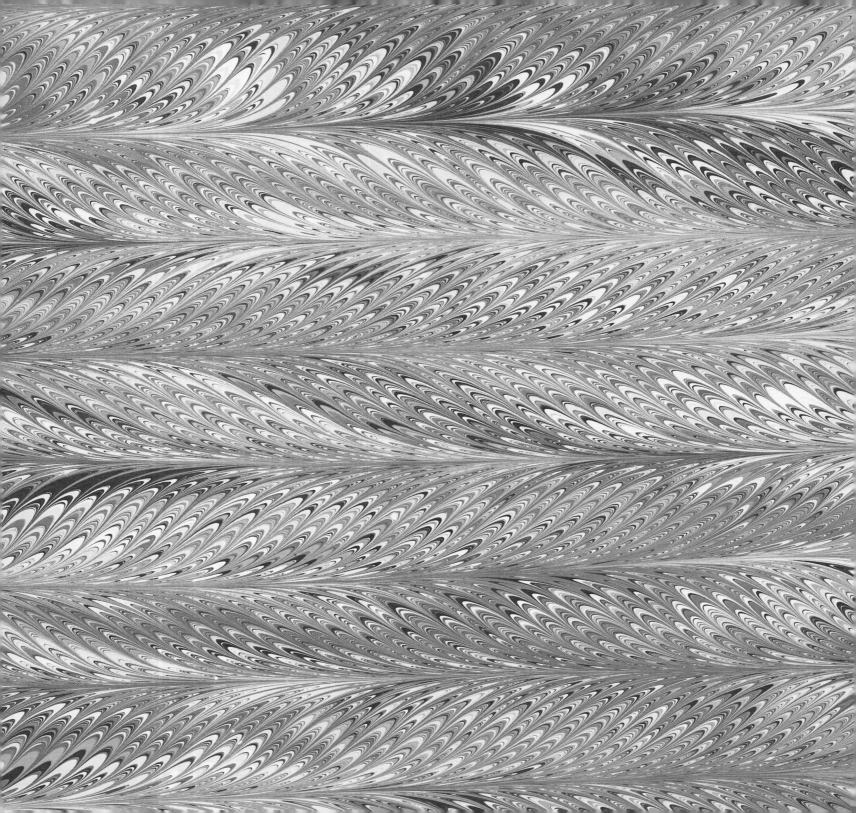